LONDON

AND THE BRITISH ISLES

Alice Taucher and Ken Bernstein

J·P·M
PUBLICATIONS

C O N T E N T S

This Way London

Melting Pot

They don't all have blue eyes, blond hair and plummy accents. One look at the streets of Great Britain's capital and you read at a glance the colorful story of a land of immigration. Ever since the 7th century, when the Venerable Bede called London "a mart of many peoples," the city has been assimilating diverse cultures. In past centuries it has welcomed such diverse groups as Jews expelled from Spain, famine-stricken Scots and Irish, French Huguenots, and Chinese dock workers. In more recent days, citizens of the old British Empire countries have streamed in to take up jobs. Today, against stiff competition, London hangs on to its title of most important financial center of Europe, and businessmen from every corner of the globe swarm to London as bees to honey. Somehow the city manages to absorb the many nationalities, customs, skin hues and accents.

Mecca of the Arts

London has always had a vibrant cultural scene, and the rich ethnic seasoning enhances the artistic stew. All the ethnic ferment goes a long way in explaining why the capital is always to the fore with the newest trends in jazz, rock and pop music.

For other visitors, it's the traditional arts that are the city's drawing card, the world-class museums, top theater productions, and equally superb opera, ballet, orchestral and chamber music.

Traditional vs. Modern

London embraces all the latest trends with enthusiasm, yet clings lovingly to the old and traditional. But the young men of the City financial district run about the streets mumbling into their mobile phones and there's nary a bowler hat and furled umbrella to be seen: time can't be made to stand still, not even in London.

Physically, too, London has been changing—a building boom has altered its face, inserting steel and glass towers amongst the Georgian and Victorian: witness Charing Cross Station or the new Lloyds building. As well, earlier attempts at the modern genre, much derided now, are being replaced or given a face-

3

A long way from traditional London: the Canary Wharf development.

lift. Meanwhile, through all the changes, light entertainment or the voice of reason—depending on how you see it—is provided by Prince Charles, who is continually reminding the architects not to go to excess.

Green Peace

Fortunately, nearly as much land in London seems to be given over to parks as to buildings. Most were acquired on behalf of the London public years ago, and are a jealously guarded privilege. You can enjoy a breather after sightseeing or shopping by stopping to feed the ducks on one of the ponds. Or have a picnic in green and pleasant surroundings. All this, right in the heart of London.

It'll be easy to strike up a conversation with the Londoner sharing your park bench, whether he's a Cockney fruit seller, a banker of old family lineage or an Indian doctor. Though they're as diverse in character as the city of villages they live in, they share a hospitable manner, and a good sense of humor. Just mention you're trying to find the British Museum, and they'll pore over your map with you to show you where to go. Some people-contact will make your London stay all the more worthwhile.

Flashback

Roman London

Julius Caesar had made reconnaissance raids on Britain a hundred years earlier, but now the Romans were serious about putting down roots. Intending to make Colchester the capital of the Britain he had newly invaded (AD 43), the Roman Emperor Claudius looked around for a Thames crossing point. He chose a site the Celtic inhabitants called Llyn-Din and dubbed it Londinium. The wooden bridge put up here was not far from modern-day London Bridge. With major roads soon radiating from the military garrison and ships calling regularly, it was inevitable that merchants would stream in and turn Londinium rapidly into one of the most prosperous towns of the Empire. Eventually it was named administrative capital of Roman Britain in place of Colchester. Around AD 200 the Romans built a strong stone wall around the town, sectioning off a semi-circular shape of about one square mile—corresponding today to the City financial district.

During the 5th century, the Romans abandoned Londinium, now much in decline as the Empire was crumbling under the attack of barbaric tribes, and the city entered a dark, confused period.

Barbarians Ahoy!

The native Celts at first welcomed the invaders—Angles, Saxons, Jutes—but then were forced to flee them. Thereafter, for a century and a half, there is no mention of Londinium in recorded history. Then we hear again of the city early in the 7th century when the first St. Paul's Cathedral was built during initial efforts to Christianize the city's intractable peoples.

In 851 Vikings sacked the city in perhaps the worst of many raids. Calm and order were intermittently restored by King Alfred and his descendants, but in 1017 the people of Lunduntown, as London was then called, had no alternative but to permit the Danish leader Canute to be crowned in their city as "king of all England."

Twin Cities

In 1060, the pious king Edward "the Confessor" took a major step in London's development by moving his court outside the walled city a mile and a half upstream. He built a new palace for himself and a minster (the forerunner of Westminster Abbey) for the monks of St. Peter. In a stroke he thus established for ever the dichotomy between the commercial City of London and the royal and administrative precinct of Westminster.

The new abbey was consecrated just a few weeks before Edward's death. William of Normandy rushed across the Channel to take charge, vanquishing the new king Harold at the Battle of Hastings (1066). William had himself crowned in style at the new abbey, and to keep watch over his new subjects ordered construction of the Tower at Thamesside.

London began to regain its former importance, attracting in the process a large number of immigrant merchants. By 1215 the nobles and merchant class had grown so strong that they were able to force King John to sign the Magna Carta, a document giving important rights to citizens and special privileges to the city of London. The Black Death of 1348 leveled them all when it unleashed a plague that made off with over half of London's population. The pestilence recurred from time to time over the next three centuries.

The Anglican Church

The influence of the Church of Rome over England came to an abrupt end in the reign of Henry VIII. The break with the Pope came over Henry's demand to divorce his first wife to marry Anne Boleyn. Rebuffed, Henry declared England independent, dissolved the monasteries and snapped up church properties. They provided him with enough funds to live up to his royal standards as well as a source of gifts for his supporters.

The country experienced a golden age under his daughter, Elizabeth I. This was the era of literary figures such as Francis Bacon, Ben Jonson, and William Shakespeare, whose plays were performed at the Globe Theatre in the rough-and-tumble suburb of Southwark across London Bridge. Under Elizabeth's tutelage, English naval supremacy was established, and her fleet brought the Spanish Armada to grief in 1588. British merchants made huge fortunes trading with the Middle East, Russia and the East Indies.

Parliament's Coup d'Etat

In the mid-17th century war broke out as the culmination of a power struggle between the Puritans of Parliament led by Oliver Cromwell and Charles I. London City merchants took the

Ludgate Hill: a red double-decker on the way to St. Paul's Cathedral.

side of Parliament, and their contributions were instrumental in defeating the Royalists. The king was beheaded and Oliver Cromwell served as Lord Protector until his death in 1658.

The monarchy was no sooner restored, under Charles II, than two great disasters descended on London. The Great Plague of 1665 wiped out one-third of the population, and a year later a great conflagration raged for several days, destroying most of the flimsy rat-infested wooden houses crowded within the city walls—the tally came to more than 13,000 dwellings and 87 churches lost.

New Face for London

For London's rebuilding, Sir Christopher Wren was thwarted in his plan to give the city some spaciousness and grandeur. He succeeded in giving London more than 50 majestic churches, but the city was rebuilt with much the same crowded medieval street pattern—though brick and stone did at least replace the inflammable timber and thatch. West on the outskirts of the original walled city, a 150-year-long building boom was just beginning. On the estates of the great landowners (today's "West End"), the first new developments of elegant terraces set around green squares sprang up, and London's elite began their exodus west.

In the 18th century, through its trade with the East and West Indies, London became one of Europe's most important commercial centers; its trade quintupled in the course of the century. It was also a brilliant cultural magnet. Literary figures such as Swift, Pope and Samuel Johnson gathered in the coffee houses and Handel composed for the royal court.

But there was another side to the coin: London was now the world's largest city, and among the poor huddled in the slums east of the City (the "East End") and south of the river, alcoholism, prostitution and crime were rife.

The thriving affairs of the Empire hit a snag when rebellion arose in the American colonies and George III was forced to let them go. As the century turned, Britain had to do battle with France as well, but the Duke of Wellington put the definitive end to Napoleon's ambitions at Waterloo.

Into the Modern Era

In 1802, four huge new docks began to handle the expanding international trade, augmented by the goods that England was churning out in the nascent Industrial Revolution. Workers streamed into London, swelling the slums; Charles Dickens documented the appalling conditions in which they lived and laboured. The Industrial Revolution also brought changes in the means of transportation: buses, trains and the world's first underground railway meant increased mobility for Londoners. New communities sprouted up around outlying subway stations and soon became an integral part of an ever greater London.

During World War I, the city was bombed by German zeppelins. But this was nothing compared to Hitler's devastating air raids, which gutted thousands of buildings in World War II. In the post-war reconstruction, highrises altered London's skyline and multi-story dwellings replaced the sordid slums.

The face of London continues to change, most prominently today in the ambitious plan to make of the vast defunct docks, doomed by container shipping, a sparkling new residential and commercial development.

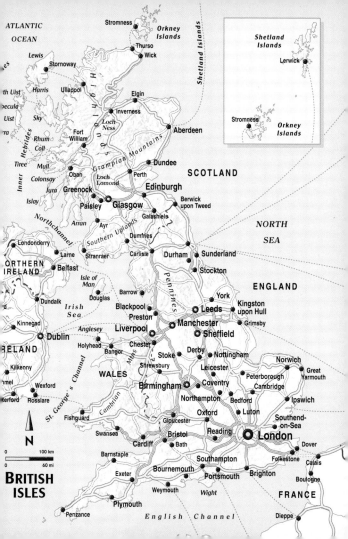

Landmarks

The easiest and often driest way to get the lie of the land is to take a tour on one of the double-decker sightseeing buses snaking their way through the city. This way, you'll be introduced to the majority of London's churches and monuments. You'll want to return, at the minimum, to the "Big Five" attractions: Buckingham Palace, the Houses of Parliament, St. Paul's Cathedral, the Tower of London, and Westminster Abbey.

❑ *THE BIG FIVE*

BUCKINGHAM PALACE

Tube: Green Park.
St. James's Park, SW1

George III must have felt that St. James's Palace was getting a bit run-down and cramped, so he leaned on the Duke of Buckingham to sell him his fine house. His son had even grander ideas, and on ascending the throne hired John Nash to improve the residence. It was still unfinished on his death, and Queen Victoria was the first to benefit from the luxurious new premises. Originally, Nash designed a U-shaped palace, with a marble arch marking the entrance to the courtyard. In 1851 a fourth side was added to the palace and the marble arch moved away to the top of Park Lane.

Of the 600 rooms in "Buck House," as Prince Charles and those in the know call it, the Queen and her consort occupy about a mere dozen, upstairs in the north wing that overlooks Green Park. Some of the royal kin also have lodgings in the palace, and the rest of the rooms are used as ceremonial salons, staff offices and domestic quarters. Sorry, you can't have tea with the Queen in her apartment, but you can—in August and September until 1997—have a look around 18 of her masterpiece-adorned ceremonial rooms, including the Throne Room and the State Dining Room. Proceeds go toward repairing fire-damaged Windsor Castle. (For information, phone 0839 1377.)

Immune to all distractions, this lavishly uniformed guard coolly puts duty first in busy Whitehall.

You can also see the Queen's horses and ceremonial coaches in the Royal Mews (open spring to fall Wed–Fri noon to 4 p.m., fall to spring Wed and Fri only) and more of her fabulous art treasures in changing exhibitions at the Queen's Gallery (Tues–Sun 9.30 a.m. to 4.30 p.m.) At 11.30 a.m. daily in summer (and on alternate days the rest of the year)—provided the weather is good—watch the colorful pageant of the Changing of the Guard that takes place in the forecourt of the Palace. The Old Guard from St. James's Palace marches up the Mall to join the Old Guard at Buckingham Palace, and the New Guard, generally accompanied by a band, arrives from Wellington Barracks via Birdcage Walk. Information. tel. 0839 123 411.

HOUSES OF PARLIAMENT (PALACE OF WESTMINSTER)

Tube: Westminster.
Parliament Square, SW1

Edward the Confessor built the first Palace of Westminster on this site in 1049 and moved the royal court here from the City. After his death William the Conqueror took it over. It remained the principal residence of the English kings for 400 years until Henry VIII acquired the Palace of Whitehall as his London home. Westminster remained ever after nonetheless the administrative center of the kingdom. The House of Lords and House of Commons sit here today. The Queen presides yearly over the State Opening of Parliament from the House of Lords; no monarch can be admitted to the House of Commons. Westminster Hall, dating from 1099, is the oldest surviving part of the Palace, most of the remainder having succumbed to fire and been rebuilt.

For admittance to the Strangers' Gallery of the House of Commons when in session (2.30–10 p.m.

WREN'S LONDON

The appearance of London owes a great debt to Sir Christopher Wren. After the Great Fire of 1666 raged for four days and nights and destroyed four-fifths of the medieval city, he was appointed surveyor general and principal architect for rebuilding it. Besides St. Paul's Cathedral, he designed 52 other churches (23 of which survived World War II's Blitz). Luckily, the flames stopped just before the Tower of London, and Westminster Abbey was far enough away not to be threatened.

Mon–Thurs, 9.30 a.m.–3 p.m. Fri), queue at St. Stephen's porch. The Prime Minister is grilled at Question Time, Tues and Thurs afternoons, drawing the biggest crowds. To improve your chances of getting in, you can apply to your embassy for a Card of Introduction. Further details: tel. 219 4272. To visit the House of Lords, apply to your embassy. Information on tel. 219 3107.

By all means, get a friend to take your photo in front of the Houses of Parliament, with the clock Big Ben towering above.

ST. PAUL'S CATHEDRAL
Tube: St. Paul's.
Ludgate Hill, EC4
Closed Sun.

This is the domed building that dominates the London skyline, the crowning achievement of England's greatest architect, Sir Christopher Wren. The cathedral is the fifth church dedicated to London's patron saint to stand on this site. When the fourth one burned down in the general conflagration, Wren found in the ashes the old center stone inscribed "Resurgam" (I shall rise again) and had the word carved on the south door pediment of his new cathedral. The edifice was the scene of the state funerals of Lord Nelson and the Duke of Wellington and the wedding of Prince Charles and Lady Diana Spencer.

The cathedral has an impressive interior, with carving by Grinling Gibbons on the choirstalls. Painters' Corner harbors the monuments of many of the great artists of the past, including Van Dyck and Constable. Go down to the crypt to view Wren's tomb, his architectural models, church vestments and other treasures, and to watch an audio-visual program that explains the cathedral's history and how it was constructed. Then climb up to the Whispering Gallery to try out its acoustics, and even higher to the Golden Gallery for a superb view of London.

REGENCY

Another architect to leave his mark on London was John Nash, who contributed a great swath of Regency terraces and circuses, extending from the northern limits of Regent's Park, down Regent Street, and on to the Mall. Upon the Regent's ascension to the throne as George IV, Nash was also involved in the costly transformation of a house once belonging to the Duke of Buckingham into Buckingham Palace.

13

'Mother of Parliaments' sprawls along the north bank of the Thames.

TOWER OF LONDON

Tube: Tower Hill.
Tower Hill, EC3
Open Mar–Oct, Mon–Sat
9 a.m.–6 p.m., Sun from 10 a.m.
Nov–Feb, closes 5 p.m.

London's number one monument in the popularity stakes. Try and get there early in the day, as there's often a long line, and avoid Sundays if you can.

The first stones were laid in the 11th century, when William the Conqueror wanted to defend his position as invading ruler. Now it's defended by colorful Yeoman Warders (the famous Beefeaters), who act as humorous and lively guides, recounting the Tower's gruesome history, and obligingly pose for photographs.

The Bloody Tower was once a prison for the likes of Anne Boleyn, Sir Thomas More and Sir Walter Raleigh, all on their way to the scaffold.

Two new events: the Jewel House showing off the fabulous Crown Jewels has been tripled in size to reduce lines, and the Palace of Edward I is open to the public for the first time ever. Costumed attendants in candle-lit rooms evoke the 13th century.

For 700 years, each evening at 9.40 p.m., the Ceremony of the Keys has taken place, whereby the Chief Warder locks the big oak doors "against the mob" to the sounding of bugles. To attend, write well ahead to: Resident Governor, Queen's House, HM Tower of London, EC3N 4AB.

WESTMINSTER ABBEY

Tube: Westminster.
Parliament Square, SW1
Entrance to the nave is free (open Mon–Sat, and Sun between services), with charges for guided tours and for visiting the choir, transepts and Royal Chapels.

This English Gothic jewel is the setting for Britain's ceremonial events—coronations (ever since William the Conqueror started the fashion in 1066), funerals of statesmen and royalty, and royal weddings. Coronations make use of the Coronation Chair at the High Altar, an old oaken throne.

The abbey is also the last resting place of many kings and queens, as well as other famous people, notably in Poets' Corner.

One of the finest monuments, that to the composer Handel, shows him holding the pages of his *Messiah*. Edward the Confessor, moving his royal court out of the old walled city, founded the abbey and the Palace of Westminster across the street, and his simple tomb lies in the heart of the abbey.

The Henry VII Chapel has a lovely fan-vaulted ceiling setting the scene for the Renaissance-style royal tombs of Henry and his mother Lady Margaret Beaufort. They are joined by Queen Elizabeth I and her half-sister Mary.

❏ *OTHER LANDMARKS*

BANQUETING HOUSE

Tube: Charing Cross.
Whitehall, SW1
Open Mon–Sat 10 a.m.–5 p.m.

The Banqueting House was built 1619–22 by Inigo Jones as an addition to Whitehall Palace, the London residence of the monarchs. The Palladian-style hall was used for a variety of court ceremonies. Its ceiling is covered by nine large pictures commissioned by Charles I from Peter Paul Rubens, who was rewarded for his efforts by a knighthood. Fourteen years later Charles was taken from this very room to be beheaded on a scaffold set up outside the house.

In 1698 the palace was burned to the ground, but the Banqueting House was spared.

CHELSEA ROYAL HOSPITAL

Tube: Sloane Square.
Royal Hospital Road, SW3
Chapel and Great Hall open
Mon–Sat 10 a.m.–noon
and 2–4 p.m., Sun from 2 p.m.
Free admission.

Charles II founded this home for elderly army veterans, who are lodged, nourished and nursed when ill. Their smart ceremonial dress is a bright scarlet uniform and three-cornered hat. The hospital is a fine Christopher Wren building, with museum, chapel and grounds. Combine your visit here with a shopping trip to King's Road.

CHISWICK HOUSE

Tube: Turnham Green, then bus
E3; or train from Waterloo.
Burlington Lane, W4
Open Apr–Oct daily 10 a.m.–6 p.m.;
Nov–Mar daily 10 a.m.–4 p.m.;
closes an hour at lunchtime

Lord Burlington, a patron of the arts and architect, built himself this Palladian-style country manor in 1725, in what was then an artistic neighborhood.
The upper floor was richly embellished with cherubs, swags and ceiling paintings by William Kent, who also designed the Italianate garden. (Chiswick is pronounced Chizzick.)

INNS OF COURT

Tube: Temple, Chancery Lane.
High Holborn, WC1

Four inns were established in the 14th century providing lodging for lawyers and law students. They make up a network of alleys and pleasant courtyard squares much like the Oxford or Cambridge colleges. Inner and Middle Temples take their name from the Knights Templar who earlier had built a church and monastery in the precinct. Magnificent 16th-century Middle Temple Hall is open to the public for short periods after 10 a.m. and 3 p.m. Mon–Fri.
Gray's Inn is the place where Shakespeare's *Comedy of Errors* was first performed (1594). Its gardens were laid out by Sir Francis Bacon with catalpa cuttings brought from America by Sir Walter Raleigh. Samuel Pepys described the gardens in his famous diary as a good place to spy on fine ladies. The gardens of Lincoln's Inn are lovelier still. At Lincoln's gatehouse, look for Henry VIII's coat-of-arms above the heavy oak doorways. Other highlights are the linenfold paneling in Old Hall, and the chapel. More legal associations on Fleet Street in the massive Victorian-Gothic edifice of the Royal Courts of Justice, where the public is admitted for viewing.

KENSINGTON PALACE

*Tube: Queensway, High Street
Kensington.
Kensington Gardens, W8
Open Mon–Sat 9 a.m.–5 p.m.,
Sun 11 a.m.–5 p.m.
Closed Sept–May (until 1998) for
renovation.*

The State Apartments are furnished
in Stuart- and Hanoverian-era
objects, highlighted by a collection of
court dress and works of art
belonging to the Queen. Some of the
royal relations have apartments in
the palace. There's a pleasant tea-
room in the Orangerie and delightful
gardens (see p. 30).

OLD BAILEY
(CENTRAL CRIMINAL COURTS)

*Tube: St. Paul's.
Old Bailey and Newgate Street, EC4
Visitors' Gallery open to the public
Mon–Fri, 10 a.m.–4 p.m., with
adjournment for lunch.
Free admission*

Watch the bewigged barristers and
judges at work. It's most fun
when a gory or scandalous case is
being tried.

SOUTHWARK CATHEDRAL

*Tube: London Bridge.
Borough High Street, SE1*

Southwark Cathedral is the fourth
church to be erected on the site.

KNOCK, KNOCK,
IT'S THE QUEEN

Temple Bar is a historic landmark
indicating the western limits of
the City. It was a simple chain between wooden posts at first, but
by 1351 a gate with prison above
it marked the spot. In the 1670s,
Christopher Wren replaced the
ensemble with a fine arch in Portland stone, and shortly afterwards
began the quaint custom of dis-
playing on it the heads of traitors.
At the end of the 19th century the
gate was replaced by a smaller
memorial to ease traffic jams.

Since the time of Elizabeth I, the
Sovereign has been required to
stop here and ask permission of
the Lord Mayor to enter the City.
He offers his official sword to the
Sovereign, who returns it, and the
symbol of state is then carried
before the royal procession to
signify that the monarch is traveling in the City limits under the
Lord Mayor's protection.

Rebuilt in Gothic style in the 13th
century, it enjoyed its heyday as
an Augustinian priory church in the
diocese of the Bishops of
Winchester. As the point of entry for
London, Southwark (pronounced
Suthurk) was an important market
town; the church gave sanctuary
to its debtors, criminals and

17

prostitutes. After the Reformation, it became run-down, and parts of it were used as a bakery and pigsties. In the 19th century the cathedral was restored to its former glory. In 1424 James I, King of Scotland, was married here to the niece of Cardinal Beaufort, Bishop of Winchester. Look for the cardinal's hat and coat-of-arms engraved on a pillar in the south transept. In Elizabethan times, the cathedral was the parish church of Shakespeare, who worked at the nearby Globe theater. There are some interesting effigies and plaques, such as the monument to John Harvard who founded Harvard University.

SPENCER HOUSE

Tube: Green Park.
27 St. James's Place, SW1
Open 11.30 a.m.–5.30 p.m. Sun
except Jan and Aug.
Princess Di's ancestor, the first Earl Spencer, built this exquisite palace in the mid-18th century. The house was leased in 1985 to one of the Rothschild companies, who have painstakingly restored it and opened it as a museum and art gallery. You can also rent the premises to throw a party, but it will cost many, many thousands of pounds. There are nine antique-filled State Rooms to visit.

ST. JAMES'S CHURCH

Tube: Piccadilly Circus.
Piccadilly, W1
The last of the London churches designed by Christopher Wren, and reputedly the one he liked best. Its highlight is the wood carving by Grinling Gibbons festooning the organ case, the font and the altarpiece. Many non-ecclesiastical activities go on here, such as a crafts market on Friday and Saturday, wholefood café, brass-rubbing center and lunchtime concerts.

ST. BRIDE'S

Tube: Blackfriars.
Fleet Street, EC4
This Christopher Wren church was once known as the "printers' church," but the printers and their newspapers have since moved away. A more lasting fame is that of inspiration for the traditional wedding cake—a pastry cook who lived in Fleet Street at the end of the 18th century became famous for his edible reproductions of the tiered steeple. Museum in the crypt.

ST. MARTIN-IN-THE-FIELDS

Tube: Charing Cross.
Trafalgar Square, WC2
Closed Sun except for services.
The lovely spires of this classical temple-style church rise over

Trafalgar Square, a little taller even than Nelson's Column. It has a long tradition as a refuge of the homeless. Free lunchtime concerts Mon, Tues and Fri at 1.05 p.m. and occasional evening concerts.

ST. JAMES'S PALACE
Tube: Green Park.
Pall Mall, SW1
Henry VIII built this red brick palace, and for 300 years it remained one of the main residences of the English monarchs. Today Prince Charles and other royal family members, including the Queen Mother, have apartments within its precincts.
The palace is connected by an overhead passage to the royal pew in Inigo Jones's Queen's Chapel; you can attend services here on Sunday from Easter to the end of July or, alternatively, at nearby Chapel Royal. The Old Guard leaves St. James's Palace daily (alternate days August to March) about 11.10 a.m. to march up the Mall to Buckingham Palace for the Changing of the Guard ceremony.

10 DOWNING STREET
Tube: Westminster.
Ever since George II presented No. 10 to Sir Robert Walpole, it has been the official residence of the prime minister. Margaret Thatcher holds the occupancy record so far.

Neighbors are the Chancellor of the Exchequer and the Party Whip, at Nos. 11 and 12. You can't get close, but have a glimpse through the gate.

TOWER BRIDGE
Tube: Tower Hill.
Open Apr–Oct daily 10 a.m.–
6.30 p.m., Nov–Mar till 5.15 p.m.
Admire the hefty drawbridges of picture-postcard Tower Bridge from the vantage point of the Tower of London—they open up (only rarely nowadays) in an incredible 90 seconds to let tall ships through. Then visit inside the bridge itself, where the exhibition The Celebration Story tells the tale of the bridge over the last 100 years.

TRAFALGAR SQUARE
Tube: Leicester Square,
Charing Cross.
Lord Nelson looks down on the square from atop his column, impervious to the traffic. Nelson was killed while he defeated the French and Spanish at the Battle of Trafalgar in 1805. It has become a tradition for political meetings and demonstrations to take place here. In the Christmas season a large tree is set up in the center of the square, a gift from Norway, and festooned with white lights, around which groups of carolers sing nightly.

19

Museums and Galleries

London has literally hundreds of museums. The British Museum, National Gallery, Natural History Museum, Science Museum, Tate Gallery and Victoria & Albert stand out in the crowd, however, and will figure on everybody's "must see" list. Their permanent collections apart, the special exhibitions that are regularly staged are reason alone to make a trip to London. (If you can pick only one, let it be the National Gallery or the British Museum.) Three of the museums are clustered together in South Kensington— the V & A, Science Museum and Natural History Museum—but they're vast, so don't try to "do" them all in one day.

❏ THE BIG SIX

BRITISH MUSEUM
Tube: Tottenham Court Road, Russell Square, Holborn.
Great Russell Street, WC1
Open Mon–Sat 10 a.m.–5 p.m., Sun 2.30–6 p.m.
Free admission.

London's largest and most famous museum, packed with treasures, including the *Magna Carta* that set out the basic tenets of English law in 1215, Egyptian mummies, the Elgin Marbles and the Sutton Hoo treasure hoard, a memorial to a 7th-century Anglo-Saxon king—it's all a bit overwhelming. The Rosetta Stone, which the French looted from Egypt and subsequently lost to the British, also resides here; it was the key to deciphering Egyptian hieroglyphics. Really riveting is the leather-like 2,000-year-old body of Lindow Man found in a waterlogged peat bog. Three new galleries have been devoted to Mesopotamian and Anatolian treasures, including some exquisite jewelry.

NATIONAL GALLERY
Tube: Charing Cross, Leicester Square.
Trafalgar Square, WC2
Open Mon–Sat 10 a.m.–6 p.m., Sun 2–6 p.m., Wed in July–Aug to 8 p.m. Free admission.

Town crier rings the bell for a Tower Hill tourist attraction.

Collections of some of the greatest European artists, in thematically arranged galleries. Leonardo da Vinci's *Virgin of the Rocks*, Rembrandt's young and old self-portraits, Turner's *Rain, Steam and Speed* and Rousseau's *Tropical Storm with a Tiger* are only a suggestion of the multitude of treasures that this museum houses. The helpful Micro Gallery is a catalog on computer; punch in the works you want to see, and it will print out a map showing where to find them. Good restaurant.

NATURAL HISTORY MUSEUM

Tube: South Kensington.
Cromwell Road, SW7
Open Mon–Sat 10 a.m.–5.50 p.m., Sun from 11 a.m.
Free admission weekdays after 4.30 p.m. and weekends after 5.

Dinosaurs, exhibits on ecology, geology and biology. Computer games, videos, interactive displays and an earthquake simulator enliven the didactic message. Everyone's heard of the extinct dodo bird, but what did it look like? The reconstruction in the Bird Gallery provides the answer. Elegant new restaurant; good educational gifts in the shop.

SCIENCE MUSEUM

Tube: South Kensington.
Exhibition Road, SW7
Open daily 10 a.m.–6 p.m. Free admission after 4.30 p.m.

One of London's most popular, visitor-friendly museums, full of old engines, veteran cars and interactive displays. It boasts a full-size replica of the Apollo 11 Lunar Lander. Among the unusual exhibits in the History of Medicine rooms are Napoleon's toothbrush and Florence Nightingale's moccasins.

ADMISSION FEES

Most museums and art galleries charge a modest admission fee, but some are free. If you plan to visit a number of the paying ones, it is worthwhile buying a London White Card, which provides entrance to 13 of the most important for a special price. Individual and family tickets (up to two adults and two children under 16) are available. The card is valid for 3- or 7-day periods and may be purchased at any of the London Tourist Board information centers or at the participating venues (which include the Museum of London, Courtauld Institute, and the V&A). There is usually no entrance fee for children under five; at some museums, discounts are offered to senior citizens and students holding an identity card.

22

TATE GALLERY

Tube: Pimlico.
Millbank, SW1
Open Mon–Sat 10 a.m.–5.50 p.m.,
Sun from 2 p.m.
Free admission.

The best of British art: from Blake, Hogarth, Stubbs, Constable and Turner (a whole wing!) to modern masters like Henry Moore and Francis Bacon. Fine restaurant and coffee shop.

VICTORIA AND ALBERT MUSEUM (V&A)

Tube: South Kensington.
Cromwell Road, SW7
Open Tues–Sun 10 a.m.–
5.50 p.m., Mon from noon
Voluntary donation.

Probably the finest decorative arts museum in the world, the V & A was the brainchild of Prince Albert; the origins go back to the Great Exhibition of 1851, celebrating the best commercial art and design of the British Empire. Dollhouses, dress collections, ceramics, furniture, jewelry, and the largest collection of Indian art outside India all find their place. The fabulous renovated Glass Gallery displays more than 6,000 objects tracing 4,000 years of glassmaking. Some of the things to seek out are the Great Bed of Ware (Ben Jonson and Shakespeare wrote about it) and the Raphael cartoon designs for tapestries for the Sistine Chapel. Good restaurant.

❏ SMALLER MUSEUMS

BANK OF ENGLAND MUSEUM

Tube: Bank.
Bartholomew Lane, EC2
Open Mon–Fri 10 a.m.–5 p.m.,
also Sun and bank holidays in
summer from 11 a.m.–5 p.m.
Free admission.

The history of the Bank is told with gold bars and plenty of banknotes among the props. Some absorbing exhibits on forgery, as well as high-tech displays illustrating how the Bank keeps track of the international money markets. Regrettably, no free samples.

BETHNAL GREEN MUSEUM OF CHILDHOOD

Tube: Bethnal Green.
Cambridge Heath Road, E2
Open Mon–Thurs and Sat
10 a.m.–5.50 p.m., Sun from
2.30 p.m.
Free admission.

This is the V & A's ode to children: the national museum of childhood. Fabulous toys, children's costumes and nursery antiques.

23

BRAMAH TEA & COFFEE MUSEUM

Tube: Tower Hill.
Clove Bldg., Maguire Street
Butlers Wharf, SE1
Open daily: 10 a.m.–6 p.m.

The story of tea and coffee is told in historical prints, pictures and maps, complemented by a collection of tea- and coffeepots. Look for the exuberant teapot in the form of the Queen, with one of her corgis serving as spout.

CABINET WAR ROOMS

Tube: Westminster.
Clive Steps, King Charles Street, SW1
Open daily Apr–Sept 9.30 a.m.–6 p.m., Oct–Mar from 10 a.m.

The basement rooms where Churchill and the War Cabinet operated during World War II, furnished as though the great man were still here, about to launch into one of his famous morale-boosting speeches.

COURTAULD INSTITUTE

Tube: Temple or Covent Garden.
Somerset House,
The Strand, WC2
Open Mon–Sat 10 a.m.–6 p.m., Sun 2–6 p.m.

The textile tycoon Samuel Courtauld put together this splendid collection of Impressionist paintings, to which other patrons added their own contributions. They are housed in a magnificent building from 1776 originally intended for important governmental offices. Among the famous works hanging here are Edouard Manet's *Bar at the Folies-Bergère* and Van Gogh's *Self-Portrait with Bandaged Ear,* plus numerous paintings by Degas, Renoir, Gauguin and Cézanne. Earlier masterpieces by Botticelli, Rubens, Dürer and Rembrandt.

DESIGN MUSEUM

Tube: Tower Hill, London Bridge.
Butlers Wharf, SE1
Open Mon–Fri 11.30 a.m.–6 p.m., Sat & Sun from noon.

This converted 1950s Docklands warehouse exhibits the best in industrial design and graphics from the 1950s to the present. On display are classic everyday objects, such as typewriters, kettles, automobiles, chairs, all by famous designers.

DICKENS'S HOUSE

Tube: Russell Square.
48 Doughty Street, WC1
Open Mon–Sat, 10 a.m.–5 p.m.

Many of Dickens's devoted readers will make their pilgrimage here to the house where he lived for two years and wrote *Oliver Twist* and several other works. Of his many London homes, this is the only one to survive.

You can see his desk, where he sat writing undisturbed by the commotion of family life going on around him. Dickens memorabilia is on display, and a shop sells his works.

DR. JOHNSON'S HOUSE
Tube: Blackfriars.
17 Gough Square off Hind Court, EC4
Open Mon–Sat, 11 a.m.–
5.30 p.m. Oct–Apr till 5 p.m.
"When a man is tired of London, he's tired of life", claimed Samuel Johnson, who lived here from 1749 to 1759. In the attic he wrote the first English dictionary, aided by six clerks. The house is furnished with Boswell's coffee cup, the tea set of his dear friend Mrs. Thrale, and portraits of Johnson and many acquaintances.

IMPERIAL WAR MUSEUM
Tube: Lambeth North, Elephant & Castle.
Lambeth Road, SE1.
Open daily 10 a.m.–6 p.m.
The definitive story of war from Flanders to the Gulf. The nightmarish London Blitz is evoked, complete with smells of burning and sounds of air sirens. You might like to try your hand at a flight simulator.

LONDON TOY AND MODEL MUSEUM
Tube: Paddington, Lancaster Gate.
21 Craven Hill, W2
Open Tues–Sat 10 a.m.–5.30 p.m., Sun from 11 a.m.
Over 3,000 toys and model trains from the 18th century to the present day. On Sundays the mini train and carousel in the garden give rides to little ones.

LONDON TRANSPORT MUSEUM
Tube: Covent Garden.
Piazza, Covent Garden, WC2
Open daily 10 a.m.–6 p.m.
Historic buses and trams, working models, and photographs: the museum traces the history of London transport from the horse-drawn carriage to the Underground system. Children can pretend to drive subway trains and buses and work train signals, and the shop sells fabulous posters.

MADAME TUSSAUD'S
Tube: Baker Street.
Marylebone Road, NW1
Open Mon–Fri 10 a.m.–5.30 p.m., Sat & Sun 9.30 a.m.–5.30 p.m.
Wax museum featuring chillingly lifelike portraits of the famous and infamous, plus a scary Chamber of Horrors. The Spirit of London ride re-creates the city over the ages

25

with all its sounds and smells. Get a combined ticket to include the adjacent Planetarium and its spectacular high-tech laser shows. This is one of London's most popular attractions, which usually means long lines. Go on a weekday, as early as possible.

MUSEUM OF LONDON
Tube: St. Paul's.
150 London Wall, EC2
Open Tues–Sat 10 a.m.–5.50 p.m.,
Sun from noon.
A fascinating survey of the history of London from prehistoric days to the present. A portion of the old Roman wall is visible through a large window, and if you ask for a Wall map, you can follow along the remaining bits outside the museum. An impressive audio-visual display recreates the Great Fire of London. The eclectic exhibits include the death mask of Oliver Cromwell, relics of the Great Plague, a 1940s air-raid shelter, and the Lord Mayor's state coach. Combine your visit here with a trip to St. Paul's Cathedral.

MUSEUM OF MANKIND
Tube: Green Park.
6 Burlington Gardens, W1
Open Mon–Sat 10 a.m.–5 p.m.,
Sun 2.30–6 p.m.
Free admission.

Pass through the Burlington Arcade from Piccadilly and you're smack in front of the museum, one of the offspring of the British Museum. Its ethnography collection may feature such things as Sioux war bonnets, Mexican turquoise mosaics, an amazing Hawaiian god made of feathers found by Captain Cook, or a Borneo longhouse—the exhibits change regularly so there's no foretelling what will be on display. Vivid re-creations of the daily life of peoples of various cultures.

MUSEUM OF THE MOVING IMAGE (MOMI)
Tube: Waterloo, Embankment.
South Bank Arts Centre, SE1
Open daily 10 a.m.–6 p.m.
History of the cinema and television. Very "hands-on" indeed—you can act out a western film or play the part of a TV newscaster, make an animated cartoon or fly like Superman. The staff includes trained actors, dressed as famous movie and TV stars.

NATIONAL PORTRAIT GALLERY
Tube: Charing Cross, Leicester Square.
St. Martin's Place, WC2
Open Mon–Sat 10 a.m.–6 p.m.,
Sun from noon.
Free admission.

Famous British faces by famous painters, including some familiar modern ones. Start on the top floor to follow chronological order. Didn't you always want to know what naughty Geoffrey Chaucer looked like? See also Henry VIII, the Brontë sisters by their brother Branwell, Princess Diana, Mrs Thatcher and hundreds more.

SHAKESPEARE'S GLOBE THEATRE AND EXHIBITION
Tube: Blackfriars/London Bridge.
New Globe Walk, Bankside, SE1
Open daily 10 a.m.–5 p.m.
The replica of Shakespeare's old Globe Theatre, complete with thatched roof, has arisen a short distance from the excavated site of the original. Guided tours show you the materials, techniques and craftsmanship that went into its re-creation. Plays are staged only in the summer months, but the planned museum and second covered theater based on a historic Inigo Jones design will attract visitors the rest of the year.

WALLACE COLLECTION
Tube: Bond Street.
Hertford House, Manchester Square, W1
Open Mon–Sat 10 a.m.–5 p.m.; Sun 2–5 p.m. Free admission.
Outstanding French paintings of the 17th and 18th centuries, Sèvres porcelain, furniture, and Frans Hals's *Laughing Cavalier.*

WELLINGTON MUSEUM (APSLEY HOUSE)
Tube: Hyde Park Corner.
149 Piccadilly, W1
Open Tues–Sun 11 a.m.–5 p.m.
The home of the first Duke of Wellington reopened in 1995 just in time to mark the 180th anniversary of the Battle of Waterloo. The duke's remarkable collection of paintings includes works by Rubens, Velazquez, Breughel, Van Dyck, Goya and others, and you can see the Waterloo Vase presented to Wellington upon his victory. In one of the rooms, immense gilt mirrors slide back to reveal a breathtaking view over Hyde Park.

WINSTON CHURCHILL'S BRITAIN AT WAR EXPERIENCE
Tube: London Bridge.
64–66 Tooley Street, SE1
Open daily 10 a.m.–5.30 p.m., Oct–Mar to 4.30 p.m.
An exploration of the effects of World War II on the lives of ordinary people, illustrating how they coped with rationing, blackouts and air-raids. The re-creation of the Blitz is frighteningly like the real thing.

27

Out and About

After your sightseeing bus tour of the city, you'd be wise to equip yourself with some comfortable shoes and set off to explore London on foot. You can easily poke around by yourself using a good map, or if you prefer, join one of the city's many organized walking tours that cover various corners of the city in fascinating detail, usually on a specific theme.

❏ PARKS AND GARDENS

Be sure to include London's parks in any of your walks—they're the city's lungs. Almost 11 percent of Greater London is green, making it the most verdant capital in the world. While some of the greenery is fenced in for the exclusive enjoyment of a square's residents—like St. James's Square—most is free for all in large public parks. Here people play ball, go boating or swimming, feed the ducks, make a soapbox speech, nap in reclining chairs, picnic on the lawn, etc. If you visit them in spring when vast expanses of daffodils are in bloom, you may never want to go home.

Topped by fanlight and sculpture, a Georgian door adds distinction to elegant Bedford Square.

BATTERSEA PARK

Bus: No. 137 from Hyde Park Corner.

A park created in the Victorian era to improve the living conditions of crowded poor districts. Ornamental lake, butterfly reserve, deer park, zoo, flower gardens. The latest addition is a Peace Pagoda donated by the Japanese.

CHELSEA PHYSIC GARDEN

Tube: Sloane Square.
66 Royal Hospital Road, SW3
Open Apr–Oct, Wed 2–5 p.m.,
Sun 2–6 p.m; daily noon to 5 p.m.
during Chelsea Flower Show.

Looking at the profusion of fragrant, colorful blooms, it's hard to realize that this lovely garden founded in 1673 was originally conceived to investigate the medicinal properties of plants. A haven of peace and beauty.

HAMPSTEAD HEATH

Tube: Hampstead, Belsize Park.
In 800 acres, everything from untamed woods to formal parkland. All this, right on the doorstep of central London. You can fly a kite, swim in a pond, fish, walk or jog, and when you're thirsty head over to the famous Spaniards Inn. Neoclassical Kenwood House at the north-east corner of the heath is open daily (free) to show off its Robert Adam library and Old Masters. Open-air concerts are held here in summer.

HYDE PARK

Tube: Marble Arch, Hyde Park Corner, Knightsbridge.
The enormous park became Henry VIII's hunting grounds after he seized the land from the monks of Westminster Abbey at the dissolution of the monasteries. Today there's boating and swimming in the Serpentine, horse riding on Rotten Row, or just an informal ball game. On Sundays, at Speaker's Corner, the Marble Arch corner of the park, advocates of every possible cause harangue the crowds gathered around.

KENSINGTON GARDENS

Tube: High Street Kensington.
Surrounding Kensington Palace are

WHERE TO WANDER

The tourist's London is normally the West End (Covent Garden, Soho, Mayfair, St. James), with forays east to visit the Tower and to South Kensington for its museums. If you have time, however, many other historic central districts are worth strolling through: Westminster and Whitehall, Bloomsbury, Chelsea, the City. Here and there, brown or blue plaques mark the houses where famous people once lived. And if you want to venture further afield, explore Hampstead, a charming hilltop village, Southwark, London's first suburb, and the Docklands area, where the old warehouses are undergoing redevelopment.

---

formal gardens originally laid out by William III: there's a pretty sunken garden, a lily pond and flowerbeds. Beyond, open parkland merges into Hyde Park, accented by the Round Pond (where weekend model yacht sailing makes a good show for children), the Italian Garden waterworks and the Albert Memorial.
The Serpentine Art Gallery shows works on the cutting edge of modern art.

REGENT'S PARK

Tube: Baker Street.

Architect John Nash won the competition supported by the Prince Regent for a park and a street linking it to Westminster. The result is Regent's Park, the terraces of Park Crescent and Outer Circle, and Regent Street. A lot to do in the park, with London Zoo, a boating lake, Queen Mary's rose garden and a summertime open-air Shakespeare theater.

ROYAL BOTANIC (KEW) GARDENS

Tube: Kew Gardens.
Kew, Richmond, Surrey

Don't think of devoting less than half a day to this delightful ensemble of gardens, conservatories and plant research facilities. Stars here are the Princess of Wales Conservatory, containing ten different tropical climates and some carnivorous plants, and the Palm House, a Victorian cast-iron greenhouse housing botanical species of the rainforest. On the grounds are Kew Palace (open to visitors), where George III lived in surprising simplicity. The estate had already been landscaped in part by Capability Brown when the king inherited it, and the monarch continued in a serious way to oversee its improvement, sending his gardener around the world with Captain Cook to find interesting plant specimens.

ST. JAMES'S PARK

Tube: Green Park, St. James's Park.

This is the oldest of the royal parks, and the prettiest. It is thought to be laid out by André le Nôtre, the landscaper of Versailles, to the order of Charles II.

Exotic wildfowl have staked their claim to the island in the park's lake, and the bridge offers great views of Buckingham Palace.

JUBILEE WALKWAY

Those with lots of energy as well as time can attempt the do-it-yourself London Silver Jubilee Walkway, comprising a 12-mile circuit that takes in most of London's historic buildings and best views. On the section running from Lambeth Bridge to Tower Bridge, it's possible to walk continuously along the river. The Jubilee Walkway is marked at intervals by panels explaining the sights. Request the free yellow map of the route at the Tourist Board.

❏ *AMUSEMENTS*

Here are a few ideas for when you
tire of museums. Children will enjoy
most of them, too.

ALIEN WAR
Tube: Piccadilly Circus.
Trocadero, 13 Coventry Street, W1
Open daily 11 a.m.–11 p.m.
Participants flee through a maze of
tunnels, led by an "armed" space
marine, with creepy aliens in hot
pursuit.

CHELSEA BRIDGE TOWER
BUNGEE JUMP
Tube: Sloane Square, then bus.
Queenstown Road, SW8
Open Thurs–Sun, 11 a.m.–5 p.m.
No admission under 14 years.
This 300-ft bungee jump guarantees
white knuckles.

DAYTONA RACEWAY
Tube: White City.
54 Wood Lane,
Shepherd's Bush, W12
Tel. 0181 749 2277
Go-karting racetrack for amateurs.
Protective clothing and a crash
helmet are provided with the
entrance ticket.

HMS BELFAST
Tube: London Bridge.
Morgan's Lane, Tooley Street, SE1

Open daily mid-Mar–Oct 10 a.m.–
6 p.m., rest of year to 5 p.m.
The warship which played an
important role in the D-Day landings
of World War II—you can board it
and explore.

LONDON BRASS RUBBING
CENTRE
Tube: Charing Cross.
St.-Martin-in-the-Fields Church,
Trafalgar Square, WC2
Open Mon–Sat 10 a.m.–6 p.m.,
Sun from noon.
Materials available to make yourself
some handsome rubbings of knights,
kings, unicorns.

LONDON DUNGEON
Tube: London Bridge.
Tooley Street, SE1
Open 10 a.m.–6.30 p.m., in winter
till 5.30 p.m.
A horror museum, not for the very
young or very sensitive. State-of-
the-art effects and waxworks give
you the creeps—torture and death,
a Jack the Ripper show and a very
realistic Great Fire.

LONDON ZOO
Tube: Camden Town.
Boat transport from Camden Lock
or Little Venice, buses 274, C2, Z1
(summer only)
Regent's Park, NW1

Open daily 10 a.m.–5.30 p.m.,
Oct–Feb till 4 p.m. or dusk .

The London Zoo opened in 1828, the first such institution in the world. Pick up a map at the main entrance and check up on feeding times, always the best entertainment. The Discover Centre organizes encounters with animals for children and puts on special shows. At the Elephant Tracking Station, you can learn how satellites are used to study movements of wild herds.

NORTH LONDON RESCUE COMMANDO

Tube: Mile End.
Cordova Road, E3
Tel. 0181 980 0289

London's biggest indoor climbing wall, with 35 routes.

QUASAR

Tube: Piccadilly Circus.
Trocadero, 13 Coventry Street, W1
Open till 1 a.m. Fri and Sat, and
midnight other nights.

Monster high-tech center for live-action laser games.

ROCK CIRCUS

Tube: Piccadilly Circus.
London Pavilion,
Piccadilly Circus, W1
Open Mon–Thurs and Sun 11 a.m.–
9 p.m., Fri & Sat till 10 p.m.

High-tech story of rock and pop, ending with Disney-style audio-animatronic® show.

TOWER HILL PAGEANT

Tube: Tower Hill.
1 Tower Hill Terrace, EC3
Open daily 9.30 a.m.–5.30 p.m.,
Nov–Mar till 4.30 p.m.

A "dark-ride" museum, where you can rest your legs while automated cars glide you past tableaux illustrating two thousand years of London life.

WEMBLEY STADIUM

Tube: Wembley Park.
British Rail: Wembley Central.
Empire Way, Wembley
Tel. 0181 902 8833
Tours daily 10 a.m.–4 p.m.,
Oct–Mar till 3 p.m.

If you're a soccer fan, you'll enjoy touring this holy of holies and pretending your team has just won the Cup. Major concerts are held here, too.

❏ *EXCURSIONS*

HAMPTON COURT PALACE

Train from Waterloo or river boat
from April to early October (takes
2 1/2–4 hours by boat).
East Molesey, Surrey

Cardinal Wolsey, who held the post of Lord Chancellor under Henry VIII, should have known better than to flaunt his wealth. In addition to that indelicacy, he proved unable to arrange a divorce for the king so that he could marry Anne Boleyn. To mark his displeasure, Henry relieved the prelate of Hampton Court—and eventually of all his other possessions.

Visitors can enjoy the Henry VIII state apartments as well as the renovated rooms of William III and Queen Caroline. The vast Tudor kitchens—the finest of their period anywhere on the globe—are set out as if a feast was in preparation. Save time to see something of the gardens, especially the famous Maze and the Great Vine planted in 1768. Adjoining Bushy Park is a vast tract of natural parkland, roamed by herds of deer.

The palace runs an outdoor son et lumière in the summer months (tel. 0181 977 7222).

Hampton Court is on London's outskirts, so reserve the better part of a day for it.

HISTORIC MARITIME GREENWICH

DLR: Island Gardens (then pedestrian tunnel under the Thames). Greenwich, SE10

Museums open daily 10 a.m.– 5 p.m.

Since the Docklands Light Railway was built, it's a cinch to reach this beautiful area a few miles downriver from central London. The historic complex is light and airy with parks, museums and, at weekends, markets. There's a great deal to see, so allot most of a day. Start by snapping a photo of Christopher Wren's breathtaking Royal Hospital, best done from the other side of the Thames. William and Mary established it for retired seamen—the counterpart of Chelsea's hospital for old soldiers. In 1873 the institution was turned into the Royal Naval College. Visitors may visit the Painted Hall—the hospital's refectory—and the chapel.

The National Maritime Museum occupies several buildings, the central part being the exquisitely restored Queen's House, built by Inigo Jones in the 17th century for Charles I's wife Henrietta Maria. Look for the Tulip Staircase and the painted bedroom ceiling. The wings to the Queen's House hold a huge collection of ships, nautical paintings and memorabilia and navigational instruments.

The Old Royal Observatory of Christopher Wren has undergone a

Lived-in castle at Windsor is a favorite day-trip destination from London.

long refurbishment, with many new features including a sound show in the Telescope Dome and a new presentation of the Greenwich Mean Time Meridian. You can stand over the line, each leg in a different hemisphere. If you're there at 1 p.m., you will see the red time ball drop on Flamsteed House's eastern turret so that ships passing can check their chronometers. The seagoing vessels *Cutty Sark* and *Gipsy Moth* are moored down at the river.

THAMES BARRIER

British Rail from Charing Cross to Charlton Station (20-minute walk)
or river boat from Westminster, Tower or Greenwich piers
Visitors' Centre: Unity Way, Woolwich, SE18
Tel. 0181 854 1373
Open Mon–Fri 10 a.m.–5 p.m., Sat & Sun 10.30 a.m.–5.30 p.m.

Huge, shiny steel fins, reminiscent of Sydney's soaring opera house, distinguish the ten gates of the globe's largest movable flood barrier, which some have called the eighth wonder of the world. The Thames tides, which in the past would rise as much as 24 feet in spring, causing horrendous flooding, are now under control. The Visitors'

35

Centre gives background information on the barrier's construction and operation, using video displays, a working model and an audio-visual show.

WINDSOR CASTLE

Train from Paddington Station or Green Line coach from Victoria (Eccleston Bridge).
Windsor, Berkshire

William the Conqueror began it all with an earth and wood fortress; subsequent monarchs upgraded it in stone, enlarged and embellished it. But it was Queen Victoria who gave the castle its present romantic all-towers-and-turrets look. It is said to be the present Queen's favorite residence, and she was much distraught when it was damaged by fire in 1992. The repairs are still underway. St. George's Chapel, where ten monarchs are buried, is a masterwork of Perpendicular Gothic of the 15th century, with delicate fan-vaulting. The State Apartments, magnificent as they are, play second fiddle to the dollhouse of Queen Mary, a palace in meticulous miniature. Windsor is on the outskirts of Greater London, so allow a day for your visit. Children will enjoy a side-trip to Legoland, accessible by shuttlebus from Windsor's train station.

EXPLORING FURTHER AFIELD

In a day-trip from London, it's possible to reach many historic places by regularly scheduled long-distance buses or trains and explore them on your own. If you prefer, book a commercial guided tour. Recorded information on day-trips: 0839 123 484.

A few suggestions:

Cambridge and **Oxford** and their great universities

Stratford-upon-Avon for a Shakespeare play and the bard's birthplace and memorabilia

Canterbury for its historic cathedral with shrine of Thomas Becket

Woburn Abbey, the 18th-century home of the Duke of Bedford, with wonderful collection of Canalettos and safari park

Hatfield House, where Queen Elizabeth I grew up

Luton Hoo, with Robert Adam's architectural finesse and gardens by Capability Brown

Salisbury for its fine Gothic cathedral and **Stonehenge,** the 5,000-year-old stone circle of the Druids nearby.

Shopping

London is the capital of shopping as well as the capital of Britain. It will take a stronger person than you to resist those enticing store windows full of merchandise from around the globe. But what you'll want to home in on assuredly are the products that carry the special British cachet.

Shops usually open Monday to Saturday 9 a.m. to 5.30 or 6 p.m. Most large stores have one late closing night a week (until 8 p.m.): Wednesdays in Knightsbridge and King's Road; Thursdays in Oxford Street, Regent Street, Covent Garden and Kensington High Street.

❏ DEPARTMENT STORES

FORTNUM & MASON
Tube: Green Park.
181 Piccadilly, W1
The firm was founded in 1707 by William Fortnum, one of Queen Anne's footmen. The sales clerks still glide over the red carpets in formal morning dress. A good place to shop for exotic comestible gifts, beautifully packaged in jars, cans and fabulous hampers. Non-edibles, too: porcelain, crystal and so on. There's also an elegant tea room.

HARRODS
Tube: Knightsbridge.
Brompton Road, SW1
Who hasn't heard of Harrods? Its 300 departments on five floors cover 20 acres. Everything you could possibly want to buy will be found here, and the services on offer can take you from your christening to your funeral. Don't miss the fabulous food halls.

LIBERTY AND CO
Tube: Oxford Circus.
210–220 Regent Street, W1
Department store famous for its distinctive printed fabrics. Their small fabric-covered items and scarves are sought-after gifts.

MARKS & SPENCER
Tube: Bond Street, Marble Arch.
458 Oxford Street, W1
Renowned for its high-quality stock— if a bit frumpy—at reasonable prices.

Men's and women's clothing, toiletries, household furnishings and select foods. Other branches on Kensington High Street and King's Road.

SELFRIDGES

Tube: Bond Street.
400 Oxford Street, W1
Vast, comprehensive department store that offers just about everything—fine fashions, household wares, electronics and a vast food hall.

❏ *FASHION AND ACCESSORIES*

AQUASCUTUM

Tube: Piccadilly Circus.
100 Regent Street, W1
Conservative, high-quality clothes for men and women featuring the best in English style. Raincoats, blazers, suits, trousers, etc.

BROWNS

Tube: Bond Street.
23–27 South Moulton Street, W1
Relaxed designer store (for men and women). Not a staid, frumpy suit in sight.

BURBERRY

Tube: Piccadilly Circus.
18 Haymarket, SW1

Mother house of the firm known for its traditional British rainwear and other tailored clothing for men and women. Their famous plaid appears on everything from scarves through coat linings to handbags.

CHURCH'S SHOES

Tube: Bond Street.
133 New Bond Street, W1
Expensive but very fine classic shoes for men and women. Other branches.

GIEVES & HAWKES

Tube: Piccadilly Circus.
1 Savile Row, W1
One of the best in made-to-measure tailoring, with a stock of ready-to-wear as well.

HARVEY NICHOLS
Tube: Knightsbridge.
Knightsbridge at Sloane Street, SW1
Four floors of the finest in fashion for men and women, plus departments of smart home furnishings and gourmet foods. Their top floor has a much-talked-about café and restaurant.

JAEGER
Tube: Piccadilly Circus.
200–206 Regent Street, W1
For the well-dressed careerwoman or -man.

JANET REGER
Tube: Knightsbridge.
2 Beauchamp Place, SW3
The ultimate in sexy silk and lace lingerie.

PEAL & CO.
Tube: Green Park.
37 Burlington Arcade, Piccadilly, W1
Cashmere, cashmere and nothing but cashmere.

RUSSELL & BROMLEY
Tube: Bond Street.
24 New Bond Street, W1
Large selection of their own-make shoes and others. High quality, elegant and expensive. Other branches.

TURNBULL AND ASSER
Tube: Piccadilly Circus
71–72 Jermyn Street, W1
If Prince Charles buys his shirts here, so can you. Made to measure or ready-to-wear, for men and women.

WESTAWAY AND WESTAWAY
Tube: Tottenham Court Road, Russell Square.
62 Great Russell Street, WC1
Stuffed to the rafters with shetlands, cashmeres and tartans. You'll never feel the cold again.

❏ *FOR THE YOUNG*

BODY SHOP
Tube: Bond Street.
372 Oxford Street, W1
Environment-conscious cosmetics chain. Many other branches.

HIT THOSE SALES!

Bargains galore are to be had during the sales, in January (some start right after Christmas) and June–July. People come from far and wide, especially for the great buys at Harrods, even camping out in the streets in advance to be at the head of the line when the doors open.

Quick turnover: taxi changes hands outside London's most famous store.

DISNEY STORE
Tube: Oxford Circus.
140–144 Regent Street, W1
Mickey, Minnie, Donald and all the gang on toys and clothing.

DR. MARTENS DEPARTMENT STORE
Tube: Covent Garden.
1–4 King Street, WC2
Mecca of the cult footwear for the young; plus clothing and accessories.

HAMLEYS
Tube: Oxford Circus.
188–196 Regent Street, W1

World's biggest toy shop, with demonstrations of new toys guaranteed to enchant parents, too.

KENSINGTON MARKET
Tube: High Street Kensington.
49–53 Kensington High Street, W8
Stalls and more stalls (indoors) of the most trendy or outrageous used clothes, shoes and accessories.

LAURA ASHLEY
Tube: Oxford Circus.
256 Regent Street, W1
Delicately flowered, pastel "granny" dresses, but also home furnishings.

NATURAL SHOE STORE
Tube: Covent Garden.
21 Neal Street, WC2
Birkenstocks and a whole range
of other clunky-but-oh-so-
comfortable shoes.

VIRGIN MEGASTORE
Tube: Tottenham Court Road.
14 Oxford Street, W1
Giant specialist in contemporary
music.

❏ ANTIQUES
Browse Bond Street, Kensington
Church Street, Portobello Road,
Pimlico Road, King's Road (west of
Edith Grove) and you'll think you
have reached nirvana.
See also Bermondsey Market, p. 43.

CHELSEA ANTIQUE MARKET
Tube: Sloane Square.
245a & 253 King's Road, SW3
String of indoor boutiques selling
granny's silver flatware or
granddad's silver-topped cane.

CHRISTIE, MANSON AND WOODS
Tube: Piccadilly Circus.
8 King Street, SW1
Famous auction house. Drop in for a
glance at whatever is due to be
auctioned.

LONDON SILVER VAULTS
Tube: Chancery Lane.
53–65 Chancery Lane, WC2
Countless silver dealers selling
antique (and modern) silver.

MALLET & SON LTD.
Tube: Bond Street.
40 New Bond Street, W1
If money were no object, you would
rush here without passing go and
buy everything in sight.

SOTHEBY'S
Tube: Bond Street.
34–35 New Bond Street, W1
Christie's big competition in the
premium-goods auction business.

❏ SPECIALTY SHOPS

ALFRED DUNHILL LTD.
Tube: Green Park.
Duke Street at Jermyn Street, W1
Havana cigars—14 kinds—are
religiously kept at 18°C and 65%
humidity. You'll also find everything
in leathergoods and menswear.

ASPREY'S
Tube: Bond Street.
165 New Bond Street, W1
Fine jewelry, fine furniture, fine
leather goods: in short, every sort of
gift item that's beautiful and pricey.

BERRY BROS. & RUDD
Tube: Green Park.
3 St. James's Street, SW1
Distinguished wine merchant,
perhaps the grandest in London.

FOYLES
Tube: Tottenham Court Road.
119 Charing Cross Road, WC1
More books than almost anywhere
in a rather chaotic multistory
institution.

GENERAL TRADING CO.
Tube: Sloane Square.
144 Sloane Street, SW1
Linens, china, crystal, furniture,
lamps—everything for the home.
The royals shop here.

HATCHARDS
Tube: Piccadilly Circus.
187 Piccadilly, W1
Bookshop landmark established 1797.
The gentleman's-library ambiance
conducive to prolonged browsing.

JAMES SMITH & SONS
Tube: Tottenham Court Road.
53 New Oxford Street, WC1
Quality umbrellas since 1830—what
could be more British?
Lots of other pointy things sold here,
too, like walking sticks, seat sticks,
and should you need one, sword-
sticks.

PAXTON & WHITFIELD
Tube: Piccadilly Circus.
93 Jermyn Street, SW1
More than 300 varieties of cheese in
this shop founded in 1797. A crock
of blue-veined Stilton would make a
great gift.

ROCOCO CHOCOLATIER
Tube: Sloane Square.
321 King's Road, SW3
Kamikaze Sticks, asparagus
look-alikes and Nipples of Venus for
chocoholics. Weightwatchers should
stay away.

THOMAS GOODE
Tube: Hyde Park Corner.
19 South Audley Street, W1
Immense selection of beautiful
china.

TWINING & CO.
Tube: Charing Cross.
216 Strand, WC2
Elegant 1706 premises for a wide
selection of teas.

❑ MARKETS
On a different plane, London's
scores of lively markets can be great
fun and offer some incredible
bargains. Listen to the stallholders'
patter, but watch out for pick-
pockets. A few of the best-known:

BERMONDSEY MARKET (NEW CALEDONIAN MARKET)
Tube: London Bridge.
Bermondsey Square, SE1
6 a.m.–2 p.m.
You must get there early, before this giant open-air antiques street market officially opens, to have the faintest chance of beating out the serious collectors and dealers in the know.

BRICK LANE, E1
Tube: Aldgate East.
Sun 5 a.m.–2 p.m.
A market with a South-Asian accent. Spices, rugs, fabrics, all to the strumming of a sitar.

BRIXTON, SW2
Tube: Brixton.
Mon–Sat, closed Wed afternoon.
Fruits and vegetables, discount clothing, records, African crafts—and the fragrant smells of West Indian food.

CAMDEN LOCK, NW1
Tube: Camden Town.
Tues–Sun.
Conglomeration of several markets, running down the high street to the canal lock. Crafts, bric-à-brac, clothes, Doc Marten shoes. The young crowd throngs here on the weekends.

COVENT GARDEN AND JUBILEE MARKETS
Tube: Covent Garden.
Covent Garden, WC2
In place of the old Covent Garden wholesale vegetable and flower market celebrated by Fielding and Hogarth is a fashionable array of shops and stands selling antiques, clothing and crafts, spilling into Jubilee Market south of the piazza. All around, lively but expensive restaurants and cafés, with daily entertainment by buskers (street musicians, jugglers, etc.).

PETTICOAT LANE
Tube: Liverpool Street, Aldgate or Aldgate East.
Middlesex Street, E1
Sun mornings.
London's legendary Sunday clothes market, now selling a bit of everything and boasting some of the most picturesque and persuasive hawkers in London.

PORTOBELLO ROAD, W11
Tube: Notting Hill Gate, Ladbrook Grove.
One of the longest street markets in Britain, trading since the 18th century. Anything and everything on Friday, antiques galore on Saturday. Antique shops clustered all around, open throughout the week.

Dining Out

London has become so cosmopolitan in its dining that it's not an easy thing to find a "typical British meal" any more. Not only does the range of its offerings—including French, Indian, Italian, Greek, Polish, Hungarian, and every shade of oriental—widen daily but the quality seems to be going up and up. Jokes about mushy Brussels sprouts are definitely antediluvian. You'll generally find a good selection of wine to accompany your meal—it's been said that the average Englishman knows more about French wine than most Frenchmen.

❏ RESTAURANTS

While London's very finest restaurants (La Tante Claire, Le Gavroche, Bibendum, etc.) are indeed praiseworthy, prices, as in any big city, are also sky high. We concentrate here on places where you can eat well without doing too much harm to your wallet.

Note that many restaurants close on the weekend, except, in general, ethnic spots.

AUBERGINE

Tube: South Kensington.
11 Park Walk, SW10
tel. 352 3449.
Closed Sat lunch & Sun.
Chic setting for a memorable gastronomic experience. On the expensive side.

BEITEDDINE

Tube: Knightsbridge.
8 Harriet Street, SW1
tel. 235 3969.
Excellent Lebanese cuisine served up by pleasant staff.

BISTROT BRUNO

Tube: Tottenham Court Road.
63 Frith Street, W1
tel. 734 4545.
Closed Sat lunch and Sun.
A trendy establishment offering robust French cuisine at reasonable prices in minimalist-style decor.

BLOOM'S

Tube: Aldgate East.
90 Whitechapel High Street, E1
tel. 247 6001.
Closed Fri evening and Sat.

Good, hearty kosher food in this Jewish institution, though you might find the atmosphere a little old-fashioned. Inexpensive.

BLUE ELEPHANT

Tube: Fulham Broadway.
4 Fulham Broadway, SW6
tel. 385 6595
Closed Sat lunch.

Jungle-like foliage sets the scene for spectacular Thai cuisine.

BLUE PRINT CAFÉ

Tube: Tower Hill.
Design Museum, Butlers Wharf, SE1
tel. 378 7031
Closed Sun evening.

Contemporary British cuisine and fabulous riverside view. Book well ahead for terrace or window seat.

BUTLERS WHARF CHOP HOUSE

Tube: Tower Hill.
Shad Thames, SE1
tel. 403 3403
Closed Sat lunch & Sun evening.

Traditional English grill restaurant at Thameside.

CAFE SPICE NAMASTE

Tube: Tower Hill.
16 Prescot Street, E1
tel. 488 9242.
Closed Sat lunch & Sun.

WHAT'S FOR BREAKFAST?

Breakfast is one institution that hasn't succumbed to Continental or other foreign influences. Traditionally it includes fried eggs and bacon, maybe sausages, fried mushrooms and tomatoes, then toast, butter and jam. This may be preceded by half a grapefruit, porridge or cornflakes. A really opulent breakfast might even include kippers or kedgeree (a curried mixture of smoked haddock, rice, mushrooms and cream).

Out-of-this world Indian cuisine in a gaily decorated setting; moderate prices.

CHURCHILL THAI KITCHEN

Tube: Notting Hill Gate.
119 Kensington Church Street, W8
tel. 792 1246.

Cheerful if crowded pub annex serving up delicious, inexpensive Thai food.

CLARKE'S

Tube: Notting Hill Gate.
124 Kensington Church Street, W8
tel. 221 9225
Closed Sat & Sun.

Delicious, sophisticated food with a Mediterranean bias, light and airy

45

dining rooms. Little choice, however, so inquire about the menu. Reservations a must.

CRANKS

Tube: Oxford Circus.
8 Marshall Street, W1
tel. 437 9431
Closed Sun.
One of a chain serving excellent vegetarian food. Inexpensive.

CRITERION

Tube: Piccadilly Circus.
224 Piccadilly, W1
tel. 930 0488.
Mid-priced brasserie with neo-Byzantine decor, run by London's star chef Marco Pierre White.

FULHAM ROAD

Tube: South Kensington.
257 Fulham Road, SW3
tel. 351 7823.
Modern British cooking at its innovative best. Luchtime set meal offers excellent value.

GEALE'S

Tube: Notting Hill Gate.
2 Farmer Street, W8
tel. 727 7969 (no booking)
Closed Sun & Mon.
Classic fish and chips joint with a permanent line waiting patiently, attesting to the tasty fare.

GREENHOUSE

Tube: Green Park.
27a Hay's Mews (off Hill St), W1
tel. 499 3331
Traditional British fare modernized by popular TV chef Gary Rhodes.

HAANDI

Tube: Warren Street.
161 Drummond Street, NW1
tel. 383 4557
Closed Sat lunch.
Very good Indian food, with the lunchtime buffet a great value.

HILAIRE

Tube: South Kensington.
68 Old Brompton Road, SW7
tel. 584 8993
Closed Sat lunch and Sun.
Intimate spot, serving imaginative gourmet food. Prefer upstairs.

KEN LO MEMORIES OF CHINA

Tube: Victoria.
67–69 Ebury Street, SW1
tel. 730 7734
Closed Sun lunch.
Excellent Chinese fare in a modern, light setting.

KENSINGTON PLACE

Tube: Notting Hill Gate.
201–205 Kensington Church Street, W8
tel. 727 3184

Delicious, modern eclectic menu served up to a yuppyish crowd at very reasonable prices.

L'ODEON

Tube: Piccadilly Circus.
65 Regent Street, W1
tel. 287 1400
Solid quality in this 200-seater. The pre-theater menu is a real bargain.

NEW WORLD

Tube: Leicester Square.
Gerrard Place, W1
tel. 734 0677
Chinatown institution. Until 6 p.m., feast on dim sum, fritters, barbecued ribs, etc. selected from carts wheeled past your table.

RIVER CAFÉ

Tube: Hammersmith (plus longish walk or short taxi ride).
Thames Wharf, Rainville Road, W6
tel. 381 8824
Closed Sun evening.
Somewhat out of the way but worth the trip for innovative Italian fare in a riverside setting.

RULES

Tube: Covent Garden, Charing Cross.
35 Maiden Lane, WC2
tel. 836 5314
Open daily noon–midnight.

RIVERSIDE DINING AND DRINKING

On a pleasant day, there's nothing nicer than a riverside meal or snack. Here are some places with Thameside seating:

Duke's Head, 8 Lower Richmond Road, SW15; tube: East Putney.

Canteen, Chelsea Harbour, SW10; bus No. 11 or 22 from Sloane Square.

Blue Print Café, see p. 45.

Pont de la Tour, Butlers Wharf, SE1; tube: Tower Hill.

Butlers Wharf Chop House, see p. 45.

People's Palace, Royal Festival Hall, SE1; tube: Waterloo.

Quayside Restaurant, 1 St . Katharine's Way, E1; tube: Tower Hill.

Doggett's Coat and Badge, 1 Blackfriar's Bridge, SE1; tube: Blackfriars.

Old Thameside Inn, Pickfords Wharf, SE1; tube: London Bridge.

Anchor Bankside, 34 Park Street, SE1; tube: London Bridge.

Founder's Arms, Bankside, SE1; tube: London Bridge.

Dickens Inn, St. Katharine's Way, E1; tube: Tower Hill.

Prospect of Whitby, 57 Wapping Wall, E1; tube: Wapping.

The Grapes, Narrow Street, E14; DLR: Westferry.

47

Head to this venerable restaurant established in 1798 for a traditional English meal. Oysters, sirloin of Scotch beef, saddle of mutton and the perfect steak-and-kidney pie.

STEPHEN BULL BISTRO

Tube: Barbican.
71 St. John Street, EC1
Tel. 490 1750
Closed Sat lunch and Sun.
Innovative cuisine, mainly French-inspired, but with desserts flying the British flag.

WODKA

Tube: High Street Kensington.
12 St. Alban's Grove, W8
tel. 937 6513
Closed at weekend lunch.
Delicate Polish cuisine and, naturally, a wide choice of vodkas.

ZAFFERANO

Tube: Knightsbridge.
16 Lowndes Street, SW1
tel. 235 5800
Closed Sun.
Top-class Italian eatery, a mid-priced gem in posh Belgravia.

❏ *TEAS AND SNACKS*

Teatime in the bustling city is possibly something only a tourist has time for, at least on a working day. In the proper British fashion, it's taken around 4 p.m. and includes a variety of sandwiches and several kinds of cakes and pastries, all washed down with pots of tea.

A "high tea" may include hot dishes, meats and salads. It's a welcome opportunity to rest after a bout of museum-visiting and can be a good alternative to dinner before a theater date.

BROWN'S BAR

Tube: South Kensington.
114 Draycott Avenue, SW3
Same café/brasserie formula as the Cambridge and Oxford outlets patronized by generations of hungry students.

BROWN'S HOTEL

Tube: Green Park.
22–24 Dover Street, W1
Tea served 3–6 p.m., no reservations taken.
A splurge, but it's worth it for the copious spread and country house atmosphere.

FORTNUM & MASON

Tube: Green Park.
181 Piccadilly, W1
A posh tea served in the St. James's Restaurant Monday to Saturday, from 3 to 5.20 p.m. No reservations taken.

GEORGIAN ROOM, HARRODS
Tube: Knightsbridge.
Fourth Floor
Brompton Road, SW1
Buffet tea from 3.30 to 5.30 p.m.

HÄAGEN-DAZS
Tube: Leicester Square.
14 Leicester Square, WC2
Also Unit 6, Covent Garden, WC2
The supreme ice cream emporium.

PATISSERIE VALERIE
Tube: Tottenham Court Road.
44 Old Compton Street, W1
Delicious French pastries for a Continental-style tea break. Larger premises at 215 Brompton Road.

PRET À MANGER
Tube: Leicester Square.
77/78 St. Martin's Lane, WC2
Best sandwich in town, sushi, salads. Other outlets of this superior snack-shop chain at 23 Fleet Street and 298 Regent Street.

RITZ HOTEL
Tube: Green Park.
Piccadilly, W1
Seatings at 3 and 4.30 p.m., Reservations essential (tel. 493 8181).
Tea—the works—in the Palm Court is a glittering if pricey affair.

❏ PUBS AND WINE BARS
Beer is the favorite in pubs and comes in a variety of types; if you don't specify what you want, you'll automatically be served bitter, which is light and clear and served at room temperature; lager is the equivalent of European beer, served chilled; stout is dark and thick, as in Guinness; mild is another dark brew. In a pub you'll get draft beer, drawn reverently before your very eyes. Shandy is half beer and half lemonade, popular with less-hardened drinkers.
Another refreshing drink is cider, available sweet, medium or dry, or mixed with blackcurrant cordial and called cider and black.
The pubs usually also sell wine, soft drinks, tea and coffee. Liquor is available but expensive.
Do carry some form of identity if you're over 18 but don't look it. You're not allowed to drink alcohol in a pub under that age.

ATLANTIC BAR & GRILL
Tube: Piccadilly Circus.
20 Glasshouse Street, W1
Though there's a restaurant, drinking in the bar is the main activity at this newcomer, popular with a style-conscious young crowd. Less plebeian than a pub and less raucous than a nightclub.

49

CITTIE OF YORK

Tube: Tottenham Court Road.
22 High Holborn, WC1
Big pub with large open fireplace
and intimate little cubicles for
confidential discussions.

ELEPHANT AND CASTLE

Tube: Vauxhall.
South Lambeth Place, SW8
Gay pub, with drag shows most
evenings. Packed to the rafters on
weekends.

FRENCH HOUSE

Tube: Piccadilly Circus.
49 Dean Street, W1
De Gaulle's Free French made this
their unofficial headquarters; it still
has a French atmosphere and French
wines are the thing to drink.

GEORGE INN

Tube: London Bridge.
77 Borough High Street, SE1
Timber-framed coaching inn with
external galleries. Outdoor seating
in the courtyard, which occasionally
serves in summer for performances
of Shakespeare.

JIMMY'S WINE BAR

Tube: High Street Kensington.
18 Kensington Church Street, W8
Live sixties and pop music. Good
food and pleasant ambiance.

KING'S HEAD PUB/THEATRE

Tube: Highbury & Islington, Angel.
115 Upper Street, N1
This is a pub with a difference—
theater performances at lunchtime
and evening. From these loins have
sprung such actors as Kenneth
Branagh and Ben Kingsley.

MUSEUM TAVERN

Tube: Tottenham Court Road.
49 Great Russell Street, WC1
Karl Marx used to tipple here when
he wanted to take a break from
writing *Das Kapital* across the
street in the British Museum reading
room.

SHERLOCK HOLMES

Tube: Charing Cross.
10 Northumberland Street, WC2
Holmes memorabilia, including
head of Hound of the Baskervilles;
upstairs a replica of 221b Baker
Street.

YE OLDE CHESHIRE CHEESE

Tube: Blackfriars.
145 Fleet Street, EC4
Closes Mon–Sat at 9.30 p.m. and
Sun after lunch.
Famous 17th-century restaurant/pub
with sawdust on the floor.
Hangout of Samuel Johnson and
Charles Dickens. Try the steak-and-
kidney pie.

Entertainment

In London you'll never be at a loss for something to do on the cultural scene. The city offers the best in opera, dance, theater, art exhibits, films and concerts. Consult the listings magazines Time Out and What's On for details or telephone Visitorcall at 0839 123 400 for the recorded message "What's On This Week".

❏ *MAJOR ARTS VENUES*

BARBICAN ARTS CENTRE
Tube: Barbican.
Barbican Centre, EC2
The London home of the Royal Shakespeare Company and the London Symphony Orchestra, the center is a veritable maze of concert halls and theaters, linked to several large residential blocks—the whole in unfriendly textured concrete. Yellow markers will help you find your way. Concerts, plays, film, art exhibitions, etc. are all represented. Pre-performance musical entertainment in the foyer, and weekend activities for children.

LONDON COLISEUM
Tube: Leicester Square.
St Martin's Lane, WC2
Home of the English National Opera, which performs in English.
Considerably less expensive than the Royal Opera House

ROYAL ACADEMY OF ARTS
Tube: Piccadilly Circus, Green Park.
Burlington House, Piccadilly, W1
Changing major art exhibitions are mounted here.
The Academy is famous for its annual Summer Exhibition, held from June to August: about a thousand artists display their works, and the public may purchase them.

ROYAL ALBERT HALL
Tube: South Kensington.
Kensington Gore, SW7
Music of all kinds is performed here, but none is more popular than the Promenade Concerts running from July to September, featuring the popular classics.

BOOKING A SEAT

Getting tickets for the more popular shows and events is never easy. The key is to book as far ahead of your visit to London as possible. Consult a London newspaper and telephone the box office directly, paying by credit card. Even for the non-blockbuster shows it's a good idea to book in advance of your visit, particularly in high tourist season. You can ask your travel agent to help.

The London Tourist Board and London Transport information centers (see pp. 91–92) can also arrange tickets or you can deal with a reputable ticket agency (such as Ticketmaster, tel. 344 4444).

If you have time and energy to spare, you may want to look for some cut-rate theater (or opera) tickets. On the morning of a performance, a limited number of reduced-price day seats are set aside for sale. Students with identification can also get cheap stand-by tickets shortly before curtain time. Come early in both cases and be prepared to stand in line. Phone Student Theatreline tel. 379 8900 after 2 p.m. to receive updates on standbys.

If you don't mind taking pot luck, The Society of West End Theatres (SWET) runs a booth in Leicester Square selling discount tickets for the day's performances. Open at noon for matinees and 1–6.30 p.m. for evening performances.

ROYAL OPERA HOUSE

Tube: Covent Garden.
Bow Street, WC2
Box office 48 Floral Street, WC2
The Royal Opera and Royal Ballet companies perform in a sumptuous red-velvet-and-gold decor.

SADLER'S WELLS THEATRE

Tube: Angel.
Rosebery Avenue, EC1
English Touring Opera performs in the spring, and visiting dance troupes the rest of the year.

SOUTH BANK CENTRE

Tube: Embankment, Waterloo.
South Bank, SE1
The biggest arts center in Western Europe consists of the National Theatre comprising three theaters (Olivier, Lyttelton, Cottesloe), three concert halls (Royal Festival, Queen Elizabeth, Purcell Room), National Film Theatre, Hayward Gallery and a film museum (MOMI). The quality of the music, theater and art at this riverside setting far outshines the forbidding concrete massiveness of

the premises. Hour-long backstage tours at the National Theatre available Monday to Saturday. Phone 633 0880 for details. Pre-performance concerts in the lobby.

❏ NIGHTCLUBS

Nightspots generally offer a regular change of music, and dress codes vary. There may also be special nights reserved for women or for gays. It's a good idea therefore to phone ahead to check the program. The famous private clubs like Annabel's are impossible to get into unless a member friend brings you or you have some pull with your hotel concierge. Following are some of the current hot addresses for music, cabaret and dancing that admit the general public.

BROWN'S
Tube: Holborn.
4 Great Queen Street, WC2
tel. 831 0802.
Check out your dancing neighbors—Tom Cruise and his like have been seen in this fairly classy place. Presentable clothes advised.

CAMDEN PALACE
Tube: Mornington Crescent.
1a Camden High Street, NW1
tel. 387 0428.

A devoted following of Brits and foreigners alike, notably for fifties and sixties music on Wednesdays.

COMEDY STORE
Tube: Piccadilly Circus.
Haymarket House, Oxendon Street, SW1
tel. 01426 914433.
Eight or nine comedians play end to end for 2 1/2 hours. Many famous British comedians got their start here.

DINGWALLS JAZZ FACTORY
Tube: Camden Town.
Middle Yard, Camden Lock, NW1
tel. 267 1999.
Legendary jazz figures as well as new stylists rub shoulders in this old converted warehouse.

EQUINOX
Tube: Leicester Square.
Leicester Square, WC2
tel. 437 1446.
The huge old Empire disco reincarnated and refurbished. State-of-the-art laser show and nine bars.

GARDENING CLUB
Tube: Covent Garden.
4 The Piazza, Covent Garden, WC2
tel. 497 3154
A different disc-jockey and different theme every evening.

Sidewalk cafés are rare, but pub clients venture outdoors on a sunny day.

GREEN ROOM, CAFÉ ROYAL

Tube: Piccadilly Circus.
68 Regent Street, W1
tel. 437 9090
Food and drinks from 7 p.m.,
show at 9 p.m. Closed Mon.
For those who would like to recapture
something of London's pre-war
cabaret scene, the Green Room
comes pretty close. An older, chic
clientele.

ICENI

Tube: Green Park.
11 Whitehorse Street, W1
tel. 495 5333
Three floors of dancing, ranging
from loud and thumping to cozy and
boudoir-like.

JAZZ CAFÉ

Tube: Camden Town.
5 Parkway, NW1
tel. 916 6000
Jazz and funk club in a converted
bank.

LIMELIGHT

Tube: Leicester Square.
136 Shaftesbury Avenue, WC2
An old church converted into a
nightclub. Enormous triptychs of the
Madonna and Child watch over the
dancing in the nave.

RONNIE SCOTT'S

*Tube: Leicester Square or
Piccadilly Circus.
47 Frith Street, W1
tel. 439 0747*

The grand-daddy of the jazz clubs of
London, where all the greats have
played.

STRINGFELLOWS

*Tube: Leicester Square.
16–19 Upper St. Martins Lane,
WC2
tel. 240 5534*

Glamorous place, with minor
celebrities occasionally to be seen
on the glass dance floor.
Dress smartly or risk being turned
away.

THE FRIDGE

*Tube: Brixton.
Town Hall Parade
Brixton Hill, SW2
tel. 326 5100*

Large, popular dance spot attracting
a multi-ethnic crowd. Go-go dancers
in cages. House and garage music
Fridays.

TALK OF LONDON

*Tube: Covent Garden, Holborn.
Parker Street, Drury Lane, WC2
tel. 0181 568 1616*

Cabaret restaurant with floorshow
and dancing.

❏ *OUTDOOR ENTERTAINMENT*

HOLLAND PARK COURT THEATRE

*Tube: High Street Kensington.
Holland Park.
Kensington High Street, W8
tel. 602 7856*

Opera, drama and dance programs
in a 600-seat outdoor facility,
protected by a canopy. The season
runs from July to August.

KENWOOD HOUSE

*Tube: Golders Green or Archway,
then bus 210.
Hampstead Lane, NW3
tel. 413 1443*

Saturday evenings in summertime,
outdoor concerts or opera on the
lawn at lakeside, occasionally with
a fireworks display.
Deck chairs are available but you
may prefer to stretch out on the
lawn. Booking essential.

REGENT'S PARK OPEN AIR THEATRE

*Tube: Baker Street or Regent's
Park.
Box office tel. 486 2431 or
486 1933*

Open-air theater from late May to
early September. Shakespeare,
Shaw and others. Book several
weeks ahead.

55

Beyond London

Beyond London is an island so rich in history, scenery and all-round charm that you'd need months to see all of its country-side, picturesque villages, stately homes, castles and cathedrals. You mustn't confuse England and Britain—and especially not when you travel to Scotland or Wales. England is the green and pleasant land anchoring the British Isles, the home of Robin Hood and Chaucer, of cricket and soccer, of Oxford and Cambridge. Shakespeare was a great Englishman, as was Winston Churchill. But Scotsmen Robert Burns, Sir Walter Scott and Robert Louis Stevenson were not. The Prince of Wales is English but Welshmen David Lloyd George, Augustus John and Dylan Thomas were not. All very touchy, even if you can understand the accents. Wherever you go, just remember to smile, drive on the left and keep an umbrella close at hand.

ENGLAND
Southern England, Central England, North Country

You may not go to England for the sunbathing, but there are fine beaches and the most thrilling seascapes. It's also a great country for hiking—the inspiring Lake District, the haunting romance of Dartmoor, the hills and gorges of the Peak District.

Quaint but real: storybook turrets loom over impeccable lawns and forests. This castle is in Scotland.

Also outdoors: the evocative monoliths of Stonehenge, the ancient ramparts of Chester, the grandiose Roman monument, Hadrian's Wall. For really rainy days, there are enough museums to last months. And you can always dry your boots and refresh your thirst in the atmosphere of a traditional pub.

For your planning purposes we divide England into three

slices, as the tourist authorities sometimes do, starting with the south.

Southern England

To the insular British returning from the Continent, the White Cliffs of **Dover** mean only one thing—home. Their dazzling whiteness, unfurling like a pennant as they come into view, has long inspired sentimental bards. Hurrying Eurotunnel customers miss the thrill.

Dover Castle, looming over the town, is a concentric fortress with 12th-century curtain walls. A network of underground tunnels burrows into the soft chalk below, so troops could be deployed unseen by the enemy. There has been a fort on this cliff since before the Roman invasion. The oldest Roman edifice in Britain (1st century) is the lighthouse, the Roman *pharos*, now a fragile crumbling ruin. Dover town tumbles out from a cleft between the cliffs. In the main street, the Roman Painted House has Britain's oldest and best preserved wall paintings. And look in at tiny St. Edmund's chapel, dating from 1253.

Sixteen miles inland from Dover through some of southeast England's most beautiful scenery, **Canterbury** was the goal of Chaucer's pilgrims. The main access to Christ Church Cathedral is through a Flamboyant Gothic gateway, built in 1517. The central tower, dominating the whole building, is a magnificent example of the Perpendicular style, the Gothic architecture developed in England in the 14th and 15th centuries. The oldest remaining part of the cathedral is the vaulted Norman crypt, the largest in England. A plaque in the Martyrdom transept marks the spot where the Archbishop of Canterbury, Thomas Becket, was murdered in 1170. Henry VIII burned Becket's remains, demolished his shrine and confiscated the cathedral's treasures.

Five south coast ports—Southampton, Portsmouth, Poole, Weymouth and Portland—were the principal launching pads for the D-Day invasion of France in 1945. **Portsmouth** has a D-Day Museum featuring the extraordinary Overlord Embroidery. The most famous warship in Portsmouth is the three-masted *HMS Victory,* flagship of Lord Nelson's fleet that sailed to the Battle of Trafalgar in 1805. England won the fateful battle but Nelson was killed. Nearby, experts are restoring an even older ship, the *Mary Rose,* salvaged from the bottom in 1982. An exhibition hall displays everyday items recovered from Henry VIII's ship.

Since Roman times, **Southampton** has been the gateway to England. It was the main port of the old Saxon kingdom of Wessex. Protected from the choppy waters of the Channel by the Isle of Wight, modern Southampton serves the luxury cruise ships and a fleet of yachts. In the Civic Centre there's a fine gallery showing British art from 1750 to the present day, as well as works of European masters and the Impressionists. In East Park there is a memorial to the 1,513 people who perished on the maiden voyage of the *Titanic*, which began festively in Southampton.

Once the hunting ground of Norman kings, the **New Forest** is a haven of peace and beauty. Ponies and deer roam the unfenced roads. In 1952 an entrepreneurial baron, Lord Montagu of Beaulieu, decreed that his stately home be turned into a pleasure park. Beaulieu, here pronounced "bewly," houses the National Motor Museum.

The least you can say about the small cathedral city of **Winchester** is that it is historic. First came the Celts, then the Romans, and then the town became the capital of King Alfred's Wessex. William the Conqueror was crowned at Winchester as well as London. Some say that Winchester was the Camelot of King Arthur; a round table linked with the legend of Arthur and his knights is on display in the Great Hall of Winchester Castle. Winchester Cathedral, begun in the 11th century on the site of the Roman forum, is said to be the largest Gothic church in Europe. Buried here is a memorable 9th-century bishop of Winchester, St. Swithin. Rain on St. Swithin's Day (July 15) is supposed to entail another 40 days of nonstop drizzle.

In the pleasant market town of **Salisbury**, the elegant spire of the medieval cathedral is England's tallest, so heavy that it tilts. The tower was added a century after the church was built (1220–65). In the north aisle you can see a 14th-century clock believed to be the oldest working clock in the world; faceless, it sounded the hours before anyone thought to design a visible representation of time.

Salisbury Plain is the site of Britain's prime prehistoric monument, **Stonehenge**. Modern-day Druids flock here, especially for the summer solstice, but day in and day out many thousands of ordinary tourists make the journey. Because of the crowds, sightseers are now kept at a distance. Even so, these mysterious Neolithic monoliths arouse awe. The construction of Stonehenge may have taken place over a thousand years, starting around 2800 BC. The Druids arrived in England much later. Many theories have been propounded about the uses of the monolithic array, but most now indicate that Stonehenge was a temple of the sun.

There's no mystery about **Bath**, an elegant little city in south-west England where the Romans enjoyed "taking the waters." For centuries after the Romans departed, the hot springs were all but forgotten. But in the early 18th century Bath became a fashionable spa. The gambler Richard ("Beau") Nash developed the resort for pleasure as well as health, and splendid architectural vistas are his monument. The social summit of Georgian Bath was the Pump Room, where the harsh-tasting hot water is still dispensed fresh from the source, as the Pump Room trio plays, lunch or tea is served.

Also in the county of Avon, **Bristol**, one of the half-dozen biggest cities in England, has many claims to fame. From here John Cabot and his son Sebastian sailed off for North America in 1497. Bristol ships played a powerful role in the wine trade, hence Bristol sherry. In more recent history, Bristol aircraft carried the flag. The home base of the famous Bristol Old Vic company is the Theatre Royal,

founded in 1766. Fans of Victorian engineering won't want to miss the Clifton Suspension Bridge over the Avon Gorge, designed by the great Isambard Kingdom Brunel.

Much of the medieval center of **Exeter** went up in smoke under the influence of World War II bombs. Miraculously, though, the low-slung cathedral was spared. This fine Gothic building, begun in 1280, is noted for its complex rib vaulting, the elaborate tracery of a huge rose window, and the crowd of sculptures on the west façade.

Southern England's most sparsely populated area, **Dartmoor**, is a national park so vast and exposed that many a hiker has gone on the missing list. Fog and marshy bogs are the usual culprits. In the middle of Dartmoor's bracing wilderness stands the notorious prison of the same name.

Entirely less sinister is the reputation of **Exmoor**, to the north, where hikers can explore tiny villages as well as sprawling moorland. Some splendid seascapes spread out from the Somerset and Devon Coast Path. Exmoor also has a place in literary history as the setting of the novel *Lorna Doone*.

Back on the south coast, **Plymouth** was the port of embarkation for the Pilgrim Fathers in

Pastel color schemes warm the charm of Brixham, on South Devon coast.

1620. It was also the home port of Sir Francis Drake. All roads lead up to the Hoe, the open green headland about the great natural harbour called the Sound. Francis Drake was playing bowls here in 1588 when news arrived that the Spanish Armada had been sighted. Drake is remembered for the confident quip, "There's plenty of time to win this game and thrash the Spaniards, too." He was right. Much of the city center was destroyed in World War II air raids, but the historic heart of Plymouth, the Barbican, was largely undamaged. Explore the narrow cobbled alleyways around Sutton Harbour and the old fish market.

The most westerly town in England, **Penzance**, is also one of the warmest spots in the country, with tropical plants flourishing and spring fields of daffodils spread above the rugged coves.

And so to **Land's End**, a granite headland jutting into the Atlantic, with waves foaming on the rocks below. This is the last stop before the Isles of Scilly and on to America.

Central England

From the Welsh Marches to the Norfolk Broads, from higher education to heavy industry,

Central England presents a thoroughly varied face—including some of the loveliest villages anywhere.

Fifty miles north of London, **Cambridge** is the smaller of England's two renowned university towns. In fact, there's not much more to Cambridge than intellectual pursuits. The learning tradition began in the 11th century in local monasteries. The papal bull officially recognizing the university was dated 1318, though effectively it was operating as early as 1200. Among the professors have been Sir Isaac Newton, Lord Tennyson and Charles Darwin. The history and architectural merit of the various college buildings make for impressive sights. By way of light relief, you can take a punt (a pole-propelled flat-bottomed boat) along the River Cam behind the medieval colleges.

The rival university, **Oxford**, is part of a sizable city of the same name, the county seat of Oxfordshire. Oxford claims to be the oldest English-speaking university in the world, with a history going back to 1167. This is the place where British prime ministers tend to come from, along with literary lights as unconventional as Percy Bysshe Shelley (expelled from University College) and Oscar Wilde. A mathematics professor, Charles Dodgson, alias Lewis Carroll, wrote *Alice in Wonderland* at Oxford. The university's 36 independent colleges are housed in modern and historic buildings, many of outstanding beauty ("the dreaming spires"). Oxford offers two priceless institutions—the Ashmolean Museum and the Bodleian Library with several million volumes.

A stately home as majestic as any royal residence, **Blenheim Palace**, a few miles north-west of Oxford, offers conducted tours. The property was a gift from Queen Anne to the first Duke of Marlborough for his victory in the Battle of Blenheim (1704). A descendant of the duke, Winston Churchill, was born here in 1874.

Scattered through the rolling hills of the **Cotswolds** are some of the country's most idyllic villages. They have names only Olde England could invent, like Bourton-on-the-Water, Stow-on-the-Wold, and Chipping Campden. The houses are constructed of beautiful honey-colored Cotswold stone or in half-timbered Tudor style. Whether you're in Upper Slaughter or Moreton-in-the-Marsh, you'll enjoy browsing, shopping and meeting the locals, taking tea or a pub lunch.

The Warwickshire town of **Stratford-upon-Avon** attracts millions of tourist-pilgrims every year, paying their respects to The

Bard. Here William Shakespeare was born and is buried, and reminders of his life and work are found on all sides. Shakespeare's Birthplace (or so tradition calls it) is next to the modern Shakespeare Centre on Henley Street. The tourist information office, at Bridge and High streets, occupies Judith Shakespeare House, where the Bard's daughter lived. The Royal Shakespeare Theatre is only one of the local venues for plays, mostly by the great man himself. Anne Hathaway's Cottage, a thatched farmhouse in nearby Shottery, is the most photogenic of the Shakespeare landmarks.

To get to the heart of the Industrial Revolution, visit **Ironbridge Gorge**, where England's first iron bridge still stands. The local inventor and bridge-builder Abraham Darby first smelted iron ore with coke in 1709. There's a museum and a big open-air museum complex.

The **Peak District** provides a wonderful breath of fresh air. Moorland for hiking, hills for climbing and streams for fishing comprise the first of England's national parks. For a change of pace, visit the villages and stately homes, most famously **Chatsworth**, the Duke of Devonshire's palatial estate, begun in the 17th century. Additions to the Baroque mansion included a sculpture gallery, theater, library and ballroom. The garden is a classic, too.

North Country

Many of the blast furnaces and slag heaps are mere memories in post-industrial northern England. The cities have cleaned up their soot-streaked buildings, and out in the country some spectacular untouched landscape awaits. Save some time for the castles and cathedrals, and Britain's Roman-era version of the Great Wall of China.

Gateway city to the north of England, **Manchester** caters to all tastes: it has eminent Victorian buildings, two world-class soccer teams, a great symphony orchestra (the Hallé), and the TV studio producing Britain's longest-running soap opera (*Coronation Street*). In the City Art Gallery, pride of place goes to local painter L.S. Lowry (1887–1976), whose landscapes and matchstick men capture the industrial north. More cheerful modern works brighten the outstanding Whitworth Art Gallery.

Chester started out as a Roman military camp and is now a thriving, modern country town with a walled old quarter on the River Dee. Its Roman and Norman ramparts are the best preserved in England, and you can walk around the town on top of them. At Newgate you can see the largest Roman amphitheater yet found in Britain.

Back in the days when it was Britain's premier seaport, **Liverpool** built opulent Victorian buildings to match its wealth and pride. With the passing of the Industrial Revolution, and a series of disasters in the cotton trade and the shipping business, the city hit the skids. The Beatles put Liverpool back on the map, the stately public buildings were restored, and the desolate docklands were turned into showplaces, walkways and waterside arcades. A highlight of the waterfront: the Merseyside Maritime Museum covers shipbuilding and emigration. Another warehouse now encompasses the Tate Gallery, Liverpool, which exchanges art with the London Tate. The Walker Art Gallery boasts one of the country's most important collections of paintings, from the 14th century to the present day. As for the Four Lads Who Shook the World, "The Beatles Story" includes a replica of the Cavern Club, where the phenomenon began.

Rail buffs flock to **York** for its expanded National Railway Museum, which documents the whole story from the 1820s. Featured are royal trains, including Queen Victoria's superluxury saloon car, and a monumental steam locomotive, the *Mallard,* which roared up to 126 mph in 1938. York's history goes back a long way before the Iron Horse. It was the headquarters of the Roman emperors, followed by Vikings and Normans. York Minster, the splendid medieval cathedral, is surrounded by narrow streets with names like Low Petergate and The Shambles. The Jorvik Viking Centre re-creates the sights, sounds and smells of 9th-century life under the Danes. The Castle Museum is a prizewinning collection of folk history with a reconstituted 19th-century street; the museum occupies the old women's prison.

Invigorating landscape awaits north of York, in the unspoiled plateau of the North York Moors. This is the heather-and-bracken setting for some of the stories of the vet James Herriot, and his TV series, *All Creatures Great and Small.* In real life the sheep are unglamorously shaggy. To hike the undulating moors you only need a love of nature and enough energy to get from one village to the next.

The **North Yorkshire coast** has some colorful and historic ports. Scarborough's Norman castle stands on the headland overlooking two bays. They've been bathing in the very chilly sea at Scarborough since the middle of the 18th century. The

Beyond the crowds on a sunny summer day in the popular Lake District.

fishing village of Robin Hood's Bay is crammed into the hillsides of a picturesque cove. Farther north, remains of a 13th-century abbey stand high above Whitby's busy harbor. The explorer James Cook learned the ropes of sailing here; the Captain Cook Memorial Museum occupies the house he once lived in.

The ever-changing sky and the breathtaking mixture of mountains, valleys and lakes draw many millions of visitors to the **Lake District**, between the Yorkshire Dales and the Irish Sea. At peak times the few roads become clogged with tourist traffic, but it's no problem to walk away from the crowds. That brooding sky, by the way, signals that this is one of England's rainiest areas, hence the fertile green tint of the stirring landscape; and sudden storms can spring up. Literary and artistic figures were enchanted by the district. The poet William Wordsworth was born at Cockermouth, went to school in the town of Windermere, and lived just outside Rydal Mount and most memorably in Dove Cottage near Grasmere. The scenery here inspired many of his works. The barn opposite the white cottage is a museum devoted to Wordsworth and his

65

friend, the poet Samuel Taylor Coleridge. Another literary footnote: Beatrix Potter, author of *Peter Rabbit,* lived at Hill Top, near the lake of Esthwaite Water. There is a Beatrix Potter Gallery at Hawkshead and The World of Beatrix Potter in Bowness. John Ruskin, the 19th-century art historian and philosopher-activist, lived in a house called Brantwood and is buried nearby in Coniston's churchyard.

Durham is the home of England's finest Norman church—a cathedral dating from the end of the 11th century. It was built on the site of a church containing the remains of St. Cuthbert, brought here in 995 by monks racing ahead of Viking raiders. St. Cuthbert's shrine is behind the high altar, and in the Galilee Chapel is the tomb of the Venerable Bede. A plaque in the cloisters mentions Prior John Washington, 15th-century ancestor of President George Washington.

Hadrian's Wall is a coast-to-coast monument to the Spanish-born Roman Emperor Hadrian (AD 76-138). No mean artist and architect, Hadrian took personal charge of the design and construction of the wall, which was intended to protect northern England—the northernmost frontier of the empire—from the barbarians in Scotland. The wall was up to 20 feet tall, with a walkway on top for sentries, and a 30-foot-deep moat on the north side. The best-preserved portions of the wall are in the middle of its 73-mile progression, near Winshields Crags, where the remains of forts and other buildings can also be seen.

SCOTLAND
Glagow, Edinburgh, The Highlands

Romantic as an ode, surprising as a bagpipe's drone, soothing as the sight of a loch in the mist, bracing as a shot of malt whisky—it all adds up to Scotland, a land of history, industry and scenery.

Scotland occupies the top third of Great Britain, of which it is a part. But Scotland keeps separate, with its own courts and laws, its own established church, banks which distribute their own banknotes—and its own distinctive accent. With a keen ear, you'll go far. And whether your name is Scottish or not, you'll find that the generosity and lively humor of this immensely talented and practical people will dispel forever the image of the dour and tight-fisted Scot.

Glasgow

Scotland's biggest city, Glasgow, used to be known for its grimy industrial face but the Victorian splendor has been restored and culture takes precedence these days. The name of Glasgow comes from Celtic, meaning "beloved green place." Here the city's founder, St. Mungo, built the first Christian church in the 6th century. Glasgow Cathedral, a fine example of pre-Reformation Gothic, was built in the 13th century on the site of St. Mungo's monastic cell. Close by is Provand's Lordship, a house built in 1470, now a museum of paintings, tapestries and furniture. The heart of Glasgow is George Square, dominated by the imposing City Chambers building. Here you'll also find the city information bureau and a dozen statues of famous people.

The Glasgow art scene is so rich that you can hardly do it justice in a day. One of Europe's outstanding collections of paintings (including works by Rembrandt, Degas, Van Gogh and Dalí) can be viewed at the Kelvingrove Park Art Gallery and Museum. And look for the marvelous Maiolica pieces dating from as early as the 16th century. Nearby, the university's Hunterian Art Gallery has more Old Masters and the definitive collection of works by James McNeill Whistler. Opened in 1983, the Burrell Collection, specially built to house the treasures collected by Scottish shipping tycoon Sir William Burrell, now steals the show in the Glasgow art world. A real Aladdin's Cave, this museum contains everything from ancient Greek and Chinese statues to Impressionist paintings.

"You tak' the high road and I'll tak' the low road…" The words of a Scottish soldier dying in a foreign land, promising his loved one a posthumous reunion on the bonnie banks of **Loch Lomond**. The anonymous lyricist has brought universal fame to the loch and its mysterious beauty. Loch Lomond, so close to Glasgow that traffic jams develop at the weekend, is the largest stretch of inland water in Great Britain. There are more than 30 islands or "inches", mostly privately owned. Water-skiing, windsurfing and para-sailing now ripple the loch's still waters, while fishing remains ever popular.

Sir Walter Scott found inspiration for his poems *Rob Roy* and *The Lady of the Lake* in the lochs, glens, crags and waterfalls of The Trossachs. This small region east of Loch Lomond summarizes all the variety and beauty of the Highlands. To be specific, it was Loch Katrine that wowed Scott, and you're unlikely to argue over

its claim to be the most romantic of Scottish lakes.

Ben Nevis, at 4,406 feet, is the highest mountain in Britain. It's a tougher climb than it looks, especially since the weather can be dangerously changeable. In fact, chances are you won't see the summit at all from the foothills, thanks to the frequent clouds. South of the mountain, Glen Coe is a popular goal for climbers and hikers. A thatch-roofed folk museum provides rainy-day refuge.

Edinburgh

The capital of Scotland, Edinburgh, has most often been described as elegant, civilized and dignified, but it's also full of surprises. Such as the easy-going atmosphere and graceful architecture more usually associated with southern Europe. For the global view, mount to Edinburgh Castle, on an extinct volcano high above the city. Two Royal Scots guards, bayonets fixed, are posted for your camera at the first gate. Tiny St. Margaret's Chapel, with its plain whitewashed interior, is the oldest building in Edinburgh and the oldest church in use in Scotland. Built by the devout Queen Margaret toward the end of the 11th century, it survived assaults that destroyed the other structures on Castle Rock. In the Palace Yard, the Great Hall, built in 1502, claims the finest hammer-beam ceiling in Britain. The oak timbers are joined without a single nail, screw or bolt. The castle's greatest treasure, the crown, scepter and sword of Scotland, are displayed in the Crown Room.

It's all downhill from Edinburgh Castle to the royal palace, Holyroodhouse, along the Golden Mile (actually 2 kilometers long). St. Giles, the High Kirk of Scotland, dominates Parliament Square. The oldest elements of the church are the four huge 12th-century pillars supporting the spire. John Knox preached here and is thought to be buried in the rear graveyard. The celebrated Palace of Holyroodhouse began life about 1500 as a mere guest residence for the adjacent, now-ruined, abbey. Except for a week or so in summer when the British Royal Family is in residence, you can take a tour of the long Picture Gallery and the King James's Tower, including the living quarters of Mary Queen of Scots.

In the 18th-century New Town of Edinburgh, Charlotte Square is reckoned to be "the noblest square in Europe"—thanks to Scottish architect Robert Adam. The National Gallery of Scotland has a distinguished collection of great painters such as Van Dyck and Velázquez, Rembrandt, Reynolds, Turner and Gainsborough.

The Highlands

In the Highlands, enjoying much of Scotland's most glorious unspoiled scenery, purple heather stretches far and wide. Ancient, rugged castles set on rocky hillsides are reflected in the still waters of the lochs. Even near the towns it's not unusual to see golden eagles or ospreys suddenly soaring up from the red-hued thicket. **Inverness** has been the capital of the Highlands since the days of the ancient Picts. One of the city's main attractions, apart from the tempting shopping possibilities, is the small modern Museum and Art Gallery in Castle Wynd. In a fascinating exhibition of Scottish Highland history from the Stone Age, you'll brush up your clan lore and see authentic dirks and sporrans, broadswords and powder horns.

Strategically sited where the **River Ness** joins the Moray Firth, Inverness is not shy about exploiting the submarine celebrity presumed to inhabit Loch Ness to the south. Boats make regular monster-spotting cruises down the loch, which is as deep as 1,000 feet—plenty of murky space for "Nessie" to elude pursuit. Sightings have been reported since the 6th century.

Picturesque **Oban**, located on the Firth of Lorn, often takes the visitor aback by its mild climate—a gift of the Gulf Stream flowing just off the coast. Roses and rhododendrons bloom here until the end of the year.

Much further north, almost at Scotland's tip, **Ullapool** nestles in a fjord landscape at Loch Broom. Now the largest village in the north-west, the community was originally founded as the point of departure for the herring-fishing industry. This is the final stop for the ferry to the Outer Hebrides. Above Ullapool, some of Scotland's most sensational scenery extends along the jagged north-west coast.

WALES
South Wales, Cardiff, North Wales

When they are not singing in enthusiastic choruses, lilting Welsh voices tell the legends of a country that goes back 6,000 years into prehistory. Here they recount the stories of the wizard Merlin and King Arthur and his sword Excalibur, of fire-blasting red dragons with devilish tails. And they ponder the magic of the Pembrokeshire "bluestones," inexplicably transported to Stonehenge on Salisbury Plain. The principality of Wales is smaller than Massachusetts but it's dramatically varied in scenery and personality—mountains, moorlands and lowlands, industrial and farm country, cliffs and sweeping beaches, castles and churches.

South Wales

If you're coming from London on the M4 motorway, you know you're in Wales as soon as you notice the inscrutable language on the bilingual road signs, full of double l's and y's and w's but so appealing to the ear. The first Welsh city you encounter, **Newport**, has links with the Arthurian legend. The Roman 2nd Legion was based near here, and archaeologists have dug into about 50 acres of ruins. Some of the highlights of their finds can be viewed at Newport's Museum and Art Gallery.

Caerphilly may be known for its white, crumbly cheese, now produced in several other towns as well. But the solid historical claim to fame is Caerphilly Castle, a classic defense system built in the days of archers and spear-throwers. Because of the marshy terrain the monumental fortress has a rather alarming tilt. It was, nevertheless, a brilliantly conceived work of 13th and 14th-century military planning.

Cardiff

The capital and metropolis of Wales, Cardiff, was once the world's number one coal-exporting port. With the closure of many Welsh coal mines, the economy has changed drastically in recent years. So has the Cardiff docks area, once notorious for its exotic characters and freewheeling nightlife. One thing that never changes is the local enthusiasm for rugby. The most electrifying event in town is any important rugby match at Arms Park. Back to history: on the site of a Roman fortification, Cardiff Castle dates from the 11th century. But it has been much improved and expanded since then, most significantly in the 19th century, with the addition of Greek, Gothic and Arabian-nights effects. The National Museum of Wales, founded in 1907, starts with Roman-era inscriptions and goes on to follow Welsh sculpture, gold and silverware and porcelain.

The cathedral in Llandaff has had a bit of bad luck over the centuries. Founded in the 12th century, it lost its roof and a tower. Cromwell's troops fed their pigs in the font. Restorations in the 19th century were doomed when the cathedral was bombed during World War II. Highlight of the postwar reconstruction: an aluminum sculpture of Christ by Sir Jacob Epstein.

Spires of Cardiff's Llandaff Cathedral, restored after wartime bombing.

The Welsh Folk Museum, in and around a castle at St. Fagans, just west of Cardiff, brings together real farmhouses and cottages, shops and mills from around the principality, going back to the 16th century.

The town of **Brecon** is an agreeable base for exploring the nearby mountains. It's big enough to have a cathedral of Norman origin (with a chapel dedicated to the shoemakers' guild) and plenty of shopping opportunities along its narrow streets. Brecon Beacons National Park is 519 square miles of hiking opportunities among pastures and gently sculpted green hills. You don't have to be a mountain-climber to reach the peak at Pen-y-Fan, altitude 2,906 feet. But before you start it's best to check in at the mountain information center four miles west of Brecon on the A470D.

Britain's only coastal national park protects the beaches, headlands, harbors and coves of Pembrokeshire. In early Wales this area was called Gwlad hud a lledrith (land of magic and enchantment), and it's still worth dreaming about. Overlooking the town of Pembroke, and almost surrounded by a river, a great castle was established in 1097. An extraordinary little town along the coast, **St. David's** is actually a cathedral city. Dedicated to the patron saint of Wales, the cathedral was built of local purple sandstone between the 12th and 14th centuries.

North Wales

The gateway to rural North Wales, **Llandudno** was developed as a beach resort during the reign of Queen Victoria. The original pier, promenade and bandstand all survive.

Rock climbers from all over Europe come to **Snowdonia National Park** to test their skills on the sheer, exposed slopes of Mt Snowdon, 3,560 feet of tough going. The original Everest expedition of Sir Edmund Hilary trained here. For maps and advice on the 840-square mile national park, stop in at one of the information offices—in the busy tourist centers of Llanberis and Betws-y-Coed.

Back on the coast, a worthy sight is **Caernarfon** and its somber 13th-century castle, standing sentinel over the Menai Strait. Caernarfon Castle is where Prince Charles was crowned Prince of Wales in 1969, following a precedent set some 600 years before by Edward of Caernarfon, eldest son of King Edward I. There is a Prince Charles Museum in the North-East Tower of the castle.

A bewilderment of passage-ways lies behind Caernarfon's massive 15-foot walls. As you work your way around, look for the Royal Welch Fusiliers Regimental Museum, a collection of military memorabilia going back to the American War of Independence.

IRELAND
Dublin, Lakes District, Galway, Connemara

Dublin

The best of Ireland is out among the bright green pastures and white stone villages, along the cliffs and beaches, rivers and bogs. But a good place to start is Dublin, a very European capital city of low-profile buildings. Many are outstanding examples of 18th-century architecture. Birthplace and inspiration of many great authors, Dublin is pervaded by contrasting moods that can affect even the transient visitor: sweeping avenues and intimate side streets, chic shopping and smokey pubs, distinguished museums and university colleges together with sports galore.

Dublin's main street is 150 feet wide and as straight as the morals of Father Theobald Mathew, the 19th-century priest known as the Apostle of Temperance. He is commemorated in one of the four monuments down the middle of **O'Connell Street**. There used to be five until the imposing Nelson Pillar, erected by the British in 1808, was demolished in 1966, in the middle of the night.

The street's best-known landmark, the General Post Office, was the command post of the 1916 Easter Rising and badly damaged in the fighting. The harsh repression of the rebels set the stage for the war of independence.

From the three-arched bridge, almost as wide as it is long, you can look up and down the River Liffey. To the east rises the copper dome of the majestic 18th-century Custom House, restored after civil war damage in 1921.

Trinity College, founded by Queen Elizabeth I in 1591, remains a timeless enclave of calm and scholarship. For centuries it was regarded as an exclusively Protestant institution. TCD, as it is generally called, is now integrated. The campus is mostly a monument to the good taste of the 18th century. You can roam the cobbled walks among trimmed lawns, fine old trees, statues and graceful stone buildings. But Trinity's greatest treasure is upstairs in the Old Library. Double-decker stacks hold thousands of books published before 1800. The prize, the Book of Kells, was handwritten and illustrated on parchment by Irish monks in the 8th or 9th century. The beauty of the script, the decoration of initial letters and words, the abstract designs, constitute the most wonderful survival from Ireland's Golden Age.

Some of Europe's finest Georgian houses face **Merrion Square**. The discreet red-brick buildings have those special Dublin doorways, flanked by columns and topped by fanlights. No two are alike. In a complex of formal buildings on the west side of the square, Dublin's largest 18th-century mansion, Leinster House, is the seat of the Irish parliament.

The **National Gallery of Ireland** displays some 2,000 works of art. Irish artists receive priority but important Dutch, English, Flemish, French, Italian and Spanish masters are also well represented. Rounding out a notable collection of medieval religious art are two glorious frescoes of the 11th or 12 cen-

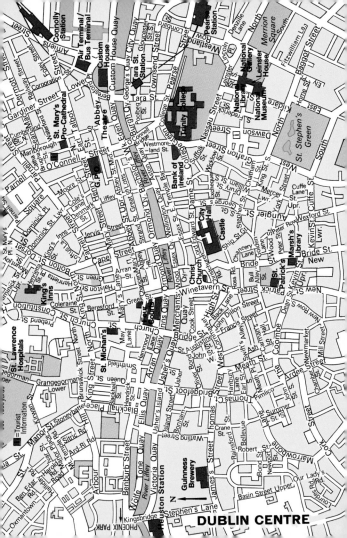

DUBLIN CENTRE

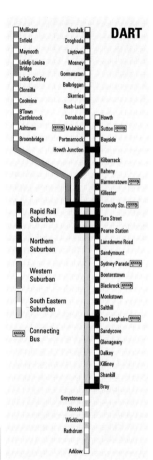

tury, originally on the walls of a chapel in Beaucaire, near Avignon, France.

The collection of the **National Museum** features the 8th-century Ardagh Chalice, the delicately worked Tara Brooch from the same era, and the Shrine of St. Patrick's Bell (12th century). You can also examine ancient Ogham stones with inscriptions in what might seem a childish way of encoding Latin. Here, too, are replicas of the greatest carved stone crosses from the early centuries of Christian Ireland.

St. Stephen's Green was almost surrounded by elegant town houses in the 18th century. A few of them still survive. Inside the square is a perfectly delightful park with flower gardens and a man-made lake inhabited by water-fowl. Among the statues is one honoring the man who paid for landscaping the park in 1880: Lord Ardilaun, son of the founder of the Guinness Brewery. Some thirsty sightseers might be inspired to find a pub and raise a toast to the stout-hearted benefactor.

Over the centuries, **Dublin Castle** has served as a seat of government, prison, courthouse, parliament, and occasionally as a fortress under siege. Begun in the 13th century on a hill overlooking the original Viking settlement, it was largely rebuilt in the 18th century.

Dublin has not one but two formidable cathedrals. And although it is the capital of a predominantly Catholic country, both cathedrals belong to the Protestant Church of Ireland. **Christ Church**, dating from 1038, has Romanesque, Early English and neo-Gothic elements. The covered pedestrian bridge over Winetavern Street, linking the church and its synod house, was built in Victorian times but doesn't spoil the overall mood.

Dublin's newer and larger cathedral, St. Patrick's, is dedicated to the national saint. It is said that **St. Patrick** himself baptized 5th-century converts at a well on this site. Jonathan Swift, the crusading satirist, was appointed dean of St. Patrick's in 1713 and served until his death in 1745. Many Swiftian relics may be seen in a corner of the north transept. The Cathedral Choir School, still in operation, was founded in 1432. A joint choir from both cathedrals was first in the world to sing Handel's *Messiah* when the composer was in Dublin in 1742.

Lakes District

The center of Ireland's lake district, **Killarney**, is a town with some lovely old churches including the 19th-century Cathedral of St. Mary in New Street and the richly decorated Parish Church of St. Mary (Church of Ireland). You can see the sights of Killarney in a variety of ways, the most picturesque being by "jaunting car," a horse-drawn rig driven by a jarvey (guide).

The scenery around the lakes —thick forests, stark crags and enchanted islands—could scarcely be more romantic. But there's adventure, too: shooting the rapids at Old Weir Bridge.

A 112-mile drive offering some truly sublime sights circles the **Ring of Kerry**. It passes among hills as steep and round as volcanoes on the way to a coast of rugged cliffs and enthralling seascapes. The first town on the route, Kenmare, is known for its lacemaking and the fish which cram its estuary. A couple of miles off the main road, north of the small resort of Castlecove, are the ruins of Staigue Fort. This 2,500-year-old stronghold, almost circular, is about 90 feet across with a wall 18 feet high. The construction and survival of such an imposing fortification was quite a feat.

A bridge now links Valentia Island, with its cliffs and tropical vegetation, to the mainland at Portmagee. The island was the European terminus of the first Atlantic cable (1866), opening telegraphic contact between the old and new worlds.

On the northern shore of the peninsula, sheer green hills plunge almost to sea-level and rocky cliffs complete the descent. Dingle Bay seems startlingly wide and the Dingle Peninsula looks like another country. Rossbeigh Strand, protected from the sea by huge sandbars, is a dream of a beach.

Five miles north of Cork, **Blarney Castle** became world famous because Queen Elizabeth I made it a common noun. The castle's owner Cormac McCarthy, the Baron of Blarney, incurred the Queen's displeasure by his delaying tactics and soothing, evasive chatter. "It is the usual blarney," the Queen is said to have despaired. And so tourists climb to the battlements, lie flat on their backs, hang on to two iron bars and extend the head down backwards to kiss the awkwardly placed stone. This may not guarantee you the gift of the gab, but it could cure your fear of heights. The castle itself, legends aside, is worth a visit, even if mighty hordes of tourists do besiege it every summer. The mighty square keep was built in the middle of the 15th century. The private park in which the castle is set includes a cool and slightly mysterious dell with ancient occult connections.

Galway

Capital of the county of the same name, Galway is a noble city and would doubtless have been even nobler if Cromwell (and later William of Orange) hadn't besieged it in the 17th century. Look first at lively Eyre Square, where John Kennedy once received a rapturous welcome.

The Collegiate Church of St. Nicholas was begun by the Anglo-Normans in 1320; note the steeple with some fine stone-carving and statuary. Near the new Cathedral, at the Salmon Weir, in June and July you can watch the salmon struggle up the narrow passage toward the sweet-water lakes—like harried passengers through a subway turnstile at rush hour.

Nearby Lynch's Castle is one of the finest town houses in Ireland, occupied today by a bank. The exterior is decorated with gargoyles, coats-of-arms and elaborate window frames. The Lynch Memorial Window recalls a 15th-century mayor who convicted and hanged his own son.

South of Galway lies County Clare, an area of wild and rugged beauty. A short distance from Ennis, the administrative capital of the county, is a weird and wonderful area, unique in Europe, the Burren. For the geology buff, this is a fascinating

The simple life: thatched cottages on Ireland's rustic Dingle Peninsula.

anomaly: a flat limestone plateau like a stony desert, worn smooth by erosion, with vertical fissures gashing the "pavement." It's a sheer delight for hikers.

Connemara

After 1654, Catholics were only permitted by their Protestant overlords to hold land west of the River Shannon, and much of that was barely inhabitable, let alone cultivable. "To Hell or Connaught" became an ironic expression, where the two alternatives were equally undesirable. The most westerly, mountainous area of Connaught, the area known as Connemara, is the least

hospitable. The sky and weather change with each gust of wind, clouds flit by and the sun darts in and out. Eighty percent of Connemara is uncultivated.

On the coast, however, the fjord-like seascapes are superb and the beaches are clean and quiet. Part of the area has been made into a national park—but it's as wild as the rest.

Clifden, the "capital" of Connemara, is little more than a two-street market town. In August local color reaches its height for the Pony Show, featuring the small, sturdy, intelligent Connemara pony.

79

Great British Food

Whether your tastes rise to gourmet heights or aim for down-to-earth pub lunches or fish and chips, you'll eat well in the British Isles. The food, everyone agrees, is better than ever. And if you should crave some international intrigue, every small town seems to have its French, Italian and Chinese restaurant. It's claimed that there are more Indian restaurants—around 5,000—in Britain than there are in India.

Many hotels start your day with a Great British breakfast. After you've packed that away, thoughts of lunch may lose their urgency. On the sightseeing trail you can grab a sandwich—or make your own from ingredients you pick up at a wayside delicatessen or food store. What could be more genuinely British than Lord Sandwich's trouble-saving 18th-century invention?

The adventure of traveling across Britain is the chance to try regional specialties—some of them so special they've barely been heard of a couple of counties away. Here are some traditional local dishes to look for.

Southern England

South of London you may run into Sussex Pond Pudding, a dessert based on suet and rich in butter and soft currants. Sussex Plum Heavies are baked raisin cakes served hot, with sugar.

Hampshire Haslet is a baked mixture of chopped pork, bread and spices. The area is also known for venison sausages from the New Forest and Hampshire Bacon Cakes with cheese added.

Westward, the pride of Cornwall, the Cornish pasty (pronounced pahss-tee), tastes better on its home ground than the mass-produced version available elsewhere around the country. A proper pasty—originally the tin miner's lunch—is a firm glazed pastry shell filled with chopped meat, onion, potato, turnip and seasoning.

In the West Country you could lose your head over a fullscale Devon cream tea with thick clotted cream; the cream is to anoint the scones or cakes that accompany the tea.

Cheddar cheese, first produced near Bath, comes from Somerset but it's available everywhere.

Central England

More cheese notes: Stilton, "the king of English cheeses," comes from the East Midlands, mostly the borders of Leicestershire and Nottinghamshire. Other Midlands cheeses are Leicester, Derby and Sage Derby.

The small town of Bakewell, in the Peak District, is the home of Bakewell pudding, a high-class cousin of the more familiar Bakewell tart, featuring almond-flavored custard and raspberry jam. It's served with cream.

North Country

Yorkshire pudding is served all over the country along with roast beef, but in Yorkshire itself the pudding usually comes first as a separate dish, drowned in onion gravy. Yorkshire is also strong on desserts—curd tarts, Yorkshire Fat Rascals, and seed cake. The Yorkshire Dales produce Wensleydale cheese, white and crumbly. Other northern cheeses are Cheshire and Lancashire. Lancashire hot-pot, a rich stew, may contain lamb or beef, onions, carrots, potatoes and mushrooms.

The north-west coast is noted for its seafood. Morecambe Bay shrimps are prized in several modes, most famously potted or in a paté, to spread on toast.

Scotland

When the Auld Alliance linked Scotland to France five centuries ago, Scotsmen began to take a serious interest in food. Since that time porridge, kippers, smoked haddock, smoked salmon, shortbread and marmalade have been exported worldwide to the further glory of Scotland.

The secret of Scottish cooking lies in the quality of the ingredients used. Aberdeen Angus cattle provide prime beef. From the icy waters of the North Sea and the North Atlantic come some of the world's finest seafood. The celebrated salmon, fresh or smoked, is now likely to come from farms—less exciting for gourmets than the wild version but more economical. Scotland is also the land of game: venison, pheasant, partridge.

If the weather's chill, start with cock-a-leekie, the national soup of Scotland, made from chicken broth, leeks and prunes. Or Scotch broth, a vegetable and mutton soup thickened with barley.

For the next course, consider stoved howtowdie wi' drapit eggs, young chicken stewed with spinach and served with poached eggs. Somewhere along the line you may be offered the mysterious haggis, which consists of sheep's innards, oatmeal, suet, onion and seasoning, sewn into a sheep's stomach bag and boiled. Eat it with chappit tatties and bashed neeps—mashed potatoes and turnips. Haggis is traditionally accompanied by whisky.

Wales

If the Welsh have a national dish, it's cawl (pronounced "cowl"), a thick and nourishing leek soup with chunks of beef and lamb or smoked ham, carrots, parsnips, potatoes and cabbage. The leek is the Welsh national emblem; on St. David's Day, men flaunt a leek in their buttonholes. Those with a sensitive sense of smell substitute a daffodil.

The locally raised lean lamb may be prepared in any number of inventive ways: baked with rosemary, cider and honey, perhaps, or roasted and served with laver sauce (a startling combination of orange juice and seaweed.) Laver, a lettuce-leaf sort of seaweed, is collected along the south coast. Boiled and mixed with oatmeal, it goes with Welsh bacon at breakfast.

Welsh rarebit (or rabbit) is known on its home ground as *caws pobi*. It's a blend of grated cheese, mustard and ale, spread on toast and browned under the grill. You're supposed to drink ale along with it.

More than 50 farmhouse cheeses are produced around Wales, which also has rich milk and butter. Local bakeries turn out breads of distinction along with baked desserts like bara brith (fruit loaf) and Welshcakes (scones).

Ireland

The Irish turn up their noses at esoteric sauces and spices. They've always liked "honest" meat and potatoes heaped high on their plates. On a blustery day, there's nothing like Irish stew, a filling casserole of lamb, potatoes, carrots, onions, parsley and thyme. The beef, too, is excellent but there is little veal. You'll have a choice of sumptuous steaks (T-bone, sirloin or filet mignon) or roast beef. Irish pork products are also famous. As for the cooking, Irish chefs have become more adventurous, winning medals on the Continent.

But to begin at the beginning, Irish breakfasts tend to be lavish spreads, with an unexpected highlight: Irish soda bread, white or brown, a real treat in itself, made of flour, buttermilk, bicarbonate of soda and salt.

Soups are usually thick and hearty: vegetables and barley and meat stock and a dab of cream, for instance. Look for potato soup made of potatoes, onions and carrots.

By the fireside in a country pub, the regulars know how to thaw out.

Fish fresh from the Atlantic or the Irish Sea or the island's streams is sensationally good. Keep an eye out for fresh salmon (poached or grilled), smoked salmon, sole, trout. Dublin prawns are a great natural resource, as are Galway oysters.

Vegetables as basic as potatoes and cabbage play a big role in Irish cooking. Potatoes have been a mainstay in the Irish diet since the 17th century. Mushrooms, which thrive in the cool and humid atmosphere, are a leading horticultural export.

Drinks. The Irish drink hundreds of millions of pints of beer a year, mostly a rich creamy dark-brown version, stout. In many a pub the laconic order, "A pint, please," means 568 milliliters of Guinness, lovingly drawn from the keg and scraped and topped. "A glass" of stout means half a pint.

The word whiskey is derived from the Gaelic *uisce beatha,* "water of life." Purists must remember to spell Irish whiskey with an "e," unlike Scotch. Pot-stilled Irish whiskey is matured in wooden casks for at least seven years. What's called the world's oldest whiskey distillery, Bushmills, has been a landmark in Northern Ireland since 1609. They run year-round tours.

83

Great British Shopping

In department stores, boutiques, street markets and country stores, shopping your way around the British Isles is all part of the adventure. The wider you travel the more you penetrate the regional quirks and charms. The sweater you buy in Scotland may be no cheaper than it would cost in London, but you'll remember the village where you found it and the smile that was included in the price.

Antiques can be rewarding anywhere in the country—in a local dealer's shop, or at a country fair. The shops are stuffed with the bric-a-brac of centuries, some of which can be had at a good price.

Aran sweaters The elaborate stitches in this Irish fisherman's sweater, knitted of undyed wool, can easily be recognized. Demand so far exceeds the supply that they are made in mainland factories as well as in the cottages of the islands of their origin. Be sure to examine the label to find out whether the Aran sweater, scarf or cap is hand-knit.

Books Beyond London's Charing Cross Road, bibliophiles know of two good sources of hard-to-get books—Blackwell's in Oxford and the Welsh border town of Hay-on-Wye.

China English bone china is unique—strong, heavy, white and translucent. Spode, Wedgwood, Minton and Royal Doulton are some of the names to seek out.

Delicacies Look for cheeses (especially blue-veined Stilton in a stout earthenware jar), teas, biscuits, Christmas puddings, jams and marmalade (the Scottish version spiked with whisky), often sold attractively gift-packed.

Fabrics Superb woollen goods and textiles in a wide range of colors and styles. Look into the competitively priced cashmere and lambswool pullovers, Shetland and Harris tweed suits as well as Viyella and Liberty offerings. Handwoven Irish tweed comes in a considerable variety of colors and weights, fit for winter overcoats or light shawls.

Convents in Limerick and County Monaghan have kept the lacemaking industry alive. Linen is woven in Northern Ireland but the finished product—from handkerchiefs to table sets—is sold all over the island.

Glassware To enhance your table setting, look for the handmade Scottish glassware by Edinburgh and Stuart Crystal and Caithness Glass. Irish Waterford crystal, world-renowned until the industry succumbed to 19th-century economic pressures, is again a going concern.

Irish souvenirs Leprechauns in all sizes, Irish coffee glasses, and shillelaghs (cudgels). Turf is now compressed and sculpted into reproductions of ancient religious and folklore symbols. Jewelry is inspired by ancient Celtic designs and illustrations from the Book of Kells. And look for reproductions of ancient Christian crosses, as well as St. Brigid crosses of straw.

Pottery Craftsmen of talent seem to gravitate to the West Country of England and to Scotland and Wales. Their handmade products can be traditional or avant-garde.

Rainwear You may need a raincoat before the vacation's over; there is no more authentic British souvenir—unless it's an umbrella.

Scottish souvenirs Bagpipes will let the neighbors know that you've been to Scotland. Or, less controversially, take home a heraldic shield or tartan proclaiming your clan. Scotch is likely to be no bargain on the spot, but you'll be able to choose among rare whiskies and fine malts that would otherwise never leave the country.

Smoked salmon If you're flying home from Dublin or Shannon, the souvenir you can eat is specially packed for traveling, on sale at the airport. So are Irish sausages and butter.

Sports equipment, such as hunting, riding and fishing gear, can't be bettered. You don't have to play the game to enjoy wearing a cricket sweater.

Victoriana In many of the industrial towns the long rows of red-brick terrace houses built for factory workers are gradually being demolished. Victorian fittings such as brass faucets and fireplace tiles, much coveted by Londoners converting old houses, are good bargains in the antique markets of towns like Manchester and Glasgow.

The Hard Facts

Babysitting

In London, most large hotels can help you with child-minding arrangements. Other avenues include Childminders (tel. 935 3000), an agency with 25 years of experience, and Universal Aunts (tel. 738 8937), another reputable firm.

Climate

Britain's weather is quite variable, so a sunny day may turn rainy, and vice versa. It's a good rule never to leave your hotel without an umbrella (a folding one is most convenient). In winter, frost and lingering snow are rarities.

Communications

Telephone. There are two area codes for London—0171 (inner area) and 0181 (outer). If calling within the same zone, it is not necessary to dial the code. In this guide, all telephone numbers have 0171 codes unless otherwise specified. To telephone abroad, dial 00 + country code + area code (without 0) + number.

Phonecards for local calls are more useful than carrying a pocketful of coins. Two companies issue them: British Telecom (BT) and Mercury; phone booths are marked for one or the other company. The cards are obtainable from post offices, newsstands and other shops. Mercury phones do not accept coins—only phonecards. Credit cards may also be used on Mercury and on some BT phones. Mercury prices are somewhat cheaper for long distance, and for either company calls are cheaper after 8 p.m. and all day Sunday.

Overseas telegrams and telemessages can be sent from any phone by dialing 190. You can send faxes from your hotel.

Post offices are normally open Mon–Fri 9 a.m. to 5.30 p.m. and until 12.30 p.m. on Saturday.

After hours, stamps are available from vending machines outside the post office, as well as from many shops.

Disabled

The disabled are well cared for in London. Artsline offers them a complimentary information and advice service on all aspects of the entertainment scene, tel. 388

Flourishing in Denbigh, Gwynedd, Wales: the Bodnant Gardens.

2227. For special accommodation, get in touch with Holiday Care Service, Imperial Bldg., Victoria Rd., Horley, Surrey, RH6 7PZ, tel. 01293 774 535.

The Airbus between Heathrow and central London is equipped to handle wheelchairs, as is the Stationlink bus connecting all the mainline stations and the Docklands Light Railway; special Mobility Buses with wheelchair access run on various routes throughout London.

Information on all the above transport is available from the Unit for Disabled Passengers, London Transport, 172 Buckingham Palace Road, London SW1 W9TN, tel. 9183312. London Transport can provide Braille maps for the visually handicapped.

Driving

Don't drive in London, if you can possibly avoid it, as parking space is practically impossible to find. Illegally parked cars may be clamped or towed away, and it is extremely expensive and time-consuming to bail them out. Parking restrictions are shown by yellow lines at roadside, and spaces provided for borough residents are strictly controlled. A parking meter, if you can find one, is usually good for a maximum of two hours. London does have some public parking lots, however, notably the 880-space facility at Park Lane at the Marble Arch traffic circle. (There is also a 24-hour gas station at 83 Park Lane.) For a free map of parking lots, contact National Car Parks, PO Box 4NH, 21 Bryanston Street, London W1A 4NH, tel. 499 7050. For theater parking, vouchers costing half the normal price are available when you book a ticket at any of the West End box offices.

There are two major 24-hour breakdown services in Britain: Automobile Association (breakdown service, tel. 0800 887766) and Royal Automobile Club (breakdown service, tel. 0800 828282). If you belong to a similar organization at home, check ahead to see if you have reciprocal privileges with them.

Car hire. Renting a car in Britain is no problem. All you need is a passport and driver's license. There may be minimum and maximum age requirements. If you pay with a credit card you avoid having to put down a big cash deposit.

Once you get the hang of driving on the left it's rather straightforward. British drivers tend to be polite, yielding the right of way much more readily than continental Europeans. As you enter a roundabout (traffic circle), give way to traffic already in the circle. At other junctions, signs or markings on the road surface normally indicate which road has priority.

Yield to pedestrians at "zebra crossings," marked by stripes on the roadway and flashing lights: they have right of way as soon as they step onto the crossing.

Britain's motorways (M1, M2 etc.) are toll-free. Important trunk roads, marked "A," have divided highways in the busy regions. Lesser roads are designated "B" and "C."

Unless otherwise announced, speed limits are 30 mph in built-up areas, 60 mph on highways and 70 mph on motorways and divided highways.

Petrol (gasoline) is measured in both Imperial gallons and liters. You can usually pay by credit card. Four-star petrol is 97 octane, three stars 94 octane and two stars 90. Unleaded 95-octane is also available.

Emergencies

If it's a matter of life or death, dial 999 (police, fire brigade or ambulance). You can dial free from any telephone and need neither coins nor a phonecard to reach the operator. Otherwise you can be treated at one of the 24-hour hospital casualty departments. Ask your hotel for the nearest or for the name of a doctor.

Free medical treatment is available from the National Health Service for citizens of the European Union and countries having reciprocal arrangements with Britain. Otherwise, you should see a private doctor for treatment and drug prescriptions. Medical Express, 117A Harley Street, London W1, tel. 499 1991, has a walk-in service. Before leaving home, check to see if your health insurance will cover you abroad. If not, it's wise to get coverage for your trip.

In London, late-opening drug stores are:

Bliss Chemist, 5 Marble Arch, tel. 723 6116, open from 9 a.m. until midnight;

Boots the Chemist, 44–46 Regent Street, tel. 734 6126, open Monday to Friday from 8.30 a.m. to 8 p.m., Saturday from 9 a.m. to 8 p.m. and Sunday from noon to 6 p.m.

Entry formalities

Visitors from outside the European Union need a passport. Citizens of the USA, Japan, and most Commonwealth and South American countries do not require a visa.

Duty-free allowances on goods purchased outside the EU and brought into the UK are (for visitors over 17 years of age): 200 cigarettes or 50 cigars or 250 grams tobacco; 2 liters wine plus 2 liters alcohol under 22% or 1 liter alcohol over 22%; 60 ml perfume and 250 ml toilet water. The allowance for goods bought in the EU is essentially whatever is reasonable for your personal consumption.

Language

The regional variations of accent and vocabulary are fascinating. If you don't understand the first time, try again. Here are a few words you'll need to know:

British	American
bill (restaurant)	check
bonnet (of car)	hood
boot (of car)	trunk
caravan	trailer
chemist's	drugstore
cul-de-sac	dead end
diversion	detour
first floor	second floor
ground floor	first floor
lift	elevator
mac	raincoat
nappy	diaper
pavement	sidewalk
petrol	gas(oline)
postbox	mailbox
queue up	stand in line
spirits	liquor
subway	underpass
tap	faucet
underground	subway

English is spoken by virtually all Irish people, but in the Gaeltacht areas of the west and south, many

89

use Gaelic on a daily basis. Don't treat it as a dialect—Gaelic is a fully-fledged language.

Lost and found

For property lost on a bus or tube, visit the London Transport Lost Property Office, 200 Baker Street, NW1. Open Mon–Fri 9.30 a.m. to 2 p.m. If you lose something in a taxi, get in touch with Taxi Lost Property Office, 15 Penton Street, N1, tel. 833 0996. Should you forget an item on the train, contact the station where your train terminated.

If you do not recover the property and wish to make a claim to your insurance company, be sure that you declare the loss to the police.

Money matters

Banks are open from 9.30 a.m. to 3.30 or 4.30 p.m., Monday to Friday, and some on Saturday morning.

Credit cards: The major ones are accepted nearly everywhere in London, though the retailer may not appreciate your charging anything less than £10. You can use credit cards such as American Express, Mastercard and Visa to get cash from ATM machines: you'll need to know your 4-digit code.

Currency: One pound (£) = 100 pence (p). Notes: £5 to £50. Coins: 1p to £1.

The Irish pound or punt (£) is divided into 100 pence. British and Irish coins are identically sized and shaped and sometimes slip across the border, but the currencies are no longer interchangeable. Coins come in denominations from 1 pence to £1, banknotes from £5 to £100.

Scotland has its own banknotes, valid in England but regarded with some suspicion by shop assistants.

Eurocheques and traveler's checks: These—as well as foreign currency—are best changed in a bank to avoid the fees of a currency exchange, hotel or shop. Be sure to have some checks in small denominations in case you run short of cash toward the end of your visit.

Public holidays

January:
    New Year's Day Bank Holiday
March or April:
    Easter holidays from Good
    Friday to Easter Monday
May:
    first and last Mondays Bank
    Holidays
August:
    last Monday Bank Holiday
December:
    25th: Christmas Day,
    26th: Boxing Day
If public holidays fall on a Sunday, the Monday is taken as a holiday.

Safety precautions

In all big cities, passports, tickets, traveler's checks and other valuables are best deposited in your hotel safe until required. Carry the necessary cash for the day and a credit card, preferably not in your wallet or handbag.

Be forewarned of the dangers that traffic poses to the pedestrian. Britain drives on the left. The situation is especially complicated in one-way streets. Be sure to read the notice printed in white at curbside at pedestrian crossings, warning either "Look left" or "Look right." Drivers are very respectful of pedestrian's rights at a crossing and generally stop as soon as they see someone waiting to cross.

Time

Britain and Ireland operate on Greenwich Mean Time (GMT) from late October until late March, when the clocks are put forward an hour.

Tipping

Attention is required in restaurants, as some automatically add 10–15 percent service charge to your check, and others leave it to you to do it. Scrutinize the menu and the check to see what the policy is—there's no point in tipping twice, although a little extra for especially good service is not amiss. No tip is required in pubs or cafeteria-style establishments. Taxi drivers and hairdressers will expect a tip of at least 10 per cent, and chambermaids and toilet attendants appreciate a small gratuity.

Toilets

Finding a public "loo" shouldn't present much of a problem, if you remember that it may be sign-posted with the initials "WC," for "water closet." They are to be found in all public buildings and parks and in many squares. At train stations, you will have to insert a coin into a turnstile. Increasingly, coin-operated "Loo-matic" toilets are to be found in cities.

Tourist information offices

British Travel Centre, 12 Lower Regent Street, Piccadilly Circus, SW1. Open daily from 9 a.m. to 6.30 p.m., with shorter hours at weekends. Information on travel throughout Britain, as well as London theater bookings.

London Tourist Board (LTB) Information Centres: Victoria Station Forecourt; Heathrow Airport Terminals 1, 2, and 3 Underground Station Concourse; Liverpool Street Station; Selfridges department store. Offices open daily (except Selfridges) from 8 or 8.30 a.m. to 6 or 7 p.m., with shorter hours at weekends.

London Transport Travel Information Centres: Victoria Euston, Liverpool Street, and King's Cross stations; tube stations at Heathrow, Piccadilly Circus, Oxford Circus. 24-hour information line: 222 1234. The information centers can also book tickets for some museums.

Tours

Bus Tours. In London, special double-decker sightseeing buses leave regularly from a number of central pick-up points, including Piccadilly Circus, Victoria, Marble Arch and Baker Street. Commentaries are given in several languages, either live or recorded. You can also do your own tour on a regular city bus: Nos. 11, 15 and 38 go past the most landmarks.

London Transport buses offer a London by Night Bus Tour, driving past the city's floodlit landmarks. Departures from Victoria Station at 7 or 9 p.m.; from Piccadilly Circus at 7.35 or 9.35 p.m.

Boat Tours. Innumerable pleasure boats ply the Thames offering commentaries of the river scene, running downstream to Greenwich, the Docklands and the Thames Flood Barrier, and upstream, from spring till fall, to Kew and Hampton Court Palace. Lunch, dinner and disco cruises are also available. Inquire at Westminster, Tower Bridge or Charing Cross piers, or check the listings magazines for details. The Tourist Board hotline number for riverboat information is 0839 123 432.

A one-day *Discoverer ticket* can be purchased at the piers entitling you to discounts on entrance fees to six riverside attractions. Tel. 987 1185 for details.

From April through September, you can also drift along historic Regent's Canal to London Zoo in a barge. Boarding points are Little Venice and Camden Lock. Information: tel. 482 2550.

Bicycle Tours. Three-hour tour of London led on weekends by the London Bicycle Tour Company, Gabriel's Wharf. Reservations: tel. 928 6838.

Walking Tours. Discover the London of Dickens, Shakespeare, the Beatles or Jack the Ripper. Walks are organized by Original London Walks (tel. 624 3978), Historical Tours (tel. 0181-668 4019) and City Walks of London (tel. 700 6931). The listings magazines give each day's program.

Transportation

Underground. Getting about London is best done by Underground (the "tube"), which is very efficient provided you avoid the weekday rush hours of 7.30 to

9.30 a.m. and 4.30 to 6.30 p.m. The tube is for Cinderella: last trains leave around midnight.

Bus. Request the All London Bus Map for Greater London at one of the information centers listed on p. 91 under Tourist Information Offices. Be sure to note details of late night buses (indicated by an "N," or an owl). Buses are no longer exclusively the two-decker red ones of old, but have been joined by other shapes and other colors.

Remember that the British are extremely polite and board buses in an orderly fashion, so take your place in the line.

Docklands Light Railway (DLR). This system of driverless trains was built in 1987 to facilitate transport in the redeveloping Docklands area. It connects with the tube system—underground at Bank and above ground at Tower Gateway (near tube station Tower Hill). If you're traveling on a single ticket, transfer from the Underground to DLR at Bank to avoid having to leave the tube network and pay a second fare. If you have a Travelcard, it's immaterial which of the two stations you change at.

Special Travel Packages. While you can always get where you're going on a single tube ticket (available in a money-saving carnet of 10 for central Zone 1) or return ticket if you plan to come back to your starting point, it will probably be more economical to buy one of the special Travelcards:

All-Zone Visitor Travelcard. A good solution if you plan to travel to the outlying corners of London every day (Heathrow, Richmond, Kew, etc.); it's available only outside of Britain through your local travel agent or agents for British Rail Intl. Available for 1, 3, 4 or 7 days, it covers all travel in all distance zones on London's Underground, buses, Docklands Light Railway and British Rail Network South East. It comes with a booklet of discount coupons for London museums. No photo required.

Off-peak Travelcard. Valid after 9.30 a.m. for 1 or 7 days or a weekend for the above-mentioned means of transport. The 7-day card requires a photo. The Travelcard is on sale at all tube stations, London Transport Travel Information Centres, and selected London newsstands, and there is a choice of distance zones at different prices. It offers the flexibility of purchasing a card for the least expensive zones 1 and 2 if you don't plan to budge from central London. Family Travelcard also available.

LT Card. Essentially the same as the Off-peak Travelcard but with no time restrictions.

Cabs. Even if you're economizing, you may have need of a taxi from time to time, particularly after a late night on the town. Drivers of the Black Cabs (now appearing in other colors as well) know every corner of the city intimately. You'll be charged the standard fare shown on the meter for any trip inside London, with supplements for luggage or extra passengers. Pick up a taxi at one of the many ranks, phone for one on 272 0272, or hail one in the street if its yellow sign is lit, indicating it's free.

Minicabs. Unlike the Black Cabs, minicabs are not licensed and may not legally solicit clients in the street. You will need to look under "minicabs" in the Yellow Pages telephone directory. Minicabs have no meters, so you should ascertain the fare before you ride, and it is well if you know the general route to be taken. Minicabs are generally cheaper than licensed taxis and indeed can be a good solution if you are, say, a group of four wishing to go to Hampton Court Palace.

In a pinch you can telephone GLH Car Service at 0181 883 5000, who have been in business for over 20 years.

Transport from Heathrow. You can board the tube to central London right at the airport (Piccadilly line). The journey takes approximately 40 minutes. Check the Journey Planner panel at the tube platform to see if and where you need to transfer to another line. A convenient but slightly more expensive solution is to board the *Airbus,* which leaves for Victoria Coach Station at 20-minute intervals, with stops along the way. It's particularly useful if you have mountains of luggage. A taxi will cost £30 to £40.

From Gatwick. The fastest way to Victoria train station is by *Gatwick Express,* a non-stop train leaving every 15 minutes. The journey takes 30 minutes. British Rail's *Thameslink* runs to King's Cross, Blackfriars and London Bridge, leaving every half-hour during the day and every hour in the evening. *Flightline 777* coach service to Victoria Coach Station takes an average of 70 minutes.

From London City Airport. Shuttle bus to Liverpool Street Station takes 25 minutes; alternatively, shuttle bus to Canary Wharf, boarding point for the DLR.

From Stansted Airport. Train to Liverpool Street Station takes about 40 minutes; National Express bus to Victoria, 80 minutes.

Long-distance coach. If you're thinking of spending a

day outside the capital, check at a London Tourist Board information center or Victoria Coach Station (164 Buckingham Palace Road, SW1, tel. 730 3499, open daily 6 a.m. to midnight) about the regularly scheduled coaches to Oxford, Cambridge, Canterbury, Brighton, etc. It's far cheaper and more reliable than the train. Tickets may be ordered by phone using a credit card.

Green Line Coaches (tel. 0181 668 7261) link central London with neighboring towns. London terminal is at Eccleston Bridge, SW1 (behind Victoria Station). Tickets sold on board.

The LTB information centers can advise you as well about guided coach tours to traditional attractions such as Stratford-on-Avon, Hampton Court Palace, Kew Gardens, etc.

Inter City Rail. For trips out of London, the mainline stations serve Britain's cities and regions as follows:

Euston for Stratford-upon-Avon, the Midlands and Glasgow. Tel. 387 7070.

King's Cross for Cambridge, York and Edinburgh. Tel. 278 2477.

Liverpool Street for Cambridge, Colchester, Ipswich and Norwich. Tel. 928 5100.

Paddington for Oxford, Bath and the West Country. Tel. 262 6767.

Victoria for Gatwick, Brighton, Canterbury and Dover. Tel. 928 5100.

Waterloo for Eurostar to continent, Winchester, Salisbury, Bournemouth and Portsmouth. Tel. 928 5100.

Stationlink buses make the circuit of all the rail stations hourly (in one direction only), seven days a week. They connect with the Airbus running between Central London and Heathrow. Brochure and information available from London Transport's information centers.

Voltage

240 volts, 50 cycle AC. Plugs are three flat prongs, so American and European appliances require an adapter. For extra security there's usually a switch on the socket.

Most hotels have a bathroom socket to accommodate two-pin 110-volt shavers.

Weights and Measures

Britain is ahead of the United States in converting to the metric system—mostly in the area of temperatures. Television forecasters talk in degrees Celsius but often translate into Fahrenheit as well. Meters and liters are used in some fields. In pubs the beer is pulled by the pint, and in the markets fruit is still sold by the pound.

95

Series editor: Barbara Ender
Text: Alice Taucher and Ken Bernstein
Layout: André Misteli
Photography: Bernard Joliat
Cartography: Falk Verlag, Hamburg